THE TRUTH
that leads to
ETERNAL LIFE

*Dedicated to the God
Who Is Gracious to
All Those Who Seek
His Life-giving Truth*

━━◗◗◗◗◗◗◗━━

CONTENTS

Unless otherwise indicated, Scripture quotations in this book are
from the modern-language *New World Translation of the Holy
Scriptures*, revised edition of 1961.

Abbreviations of names of other Bible versions quoted:

AT - The Bible: An American Translation, by J. Smith and
       E. Goodspeed, of 1935.

AV - Authorized or King James Version Bible, of 1611.

Dy - Roman Catholic Douay Version, of 1610.

"God . . . will wipe out every tear from their eyes, and death will be no more, neither will mourning nor outcry nor pain be any more."—Rev. 21:3, 4.

CHAPTER 1

Grand Blessings from God Near at Hand!

DO YOU want to live in peace and happiness? Do you desire good health and long life for yourself and your loved ones? Do you long to see wickedness and suffering end? Every honest-hearted person wants these things. But today, in all parts of the earth, violence, crime, hunger and sickness are increasing. Why is the world so filled with trouble? What does it all mean? Is there any sound reason to believe that conditions will really get better in our lifetime?

[2] Yes, there is reason for such hope, and it is clearly set out in a book that is published in more languages than any other book in the world. That book is the Bible. It tells us of God's purpose to set up an entirely new system of things for mankind. If you had the power to do so, would you not bring to an end the conditions that cause so much sorrow? Of course you would! Should we think that the Creator of mankind will do any less? The Bible tells us that "God is love." (1 John 4:8) Surely this loving heavenly Father knows what mankind needs. He has the power to fill those needs, and he will most certainly do so, for Psalm

1. In view of worsening world conditions, what questions arise?
2. (a) What book gives us reason for hope? (b) Why can we reasonably think that the loving Creator will bring an end to conditions that cause sorrow?

5

145:16* says of God: "You are opening your hand and satisfying the desire of every living thing." —See also Deuteronomy 32:4.

³ When will God satisfy man's desire for true peace and happiness, along with lasting health and life? Must mankind wait for thousands of years more? No! The time is near at hand! But how can this be? Conditions in the world are getting worse, not better. True, but the Bible clearly showed, long in advance, that these very conditions would be proof that we are living in the "last days" of the present wicked system. (2 Timothy 3:1-5) Soon the loving Creator will bring to their end both wickedness and those who cause it. But God will richly bless honest-hearted ones who want to do what is right, for he promises: "The world is passing away and so is its desire, but he that does the will of God remains forever." —1 John 2:17.

WHAT GOD WILL DO FOR MANKIND

⁴ What a change this earth will experience! There will be no more war, nor will there be any of the suffering that war brings. Hatred, selfishness, crime and violence will all be things of the past. Instead, there will be perfect peace and security on earth. God's own Word declares: "Just a little while longer, and the wicked one will be no more; . . . the meek ones themselves will possess the earth, and they will indeed find their exquisite delight in the abundance of peace." (Psalm 37:10, 11 [36:10, 11, *Dy*]) Such peace will exist, not only

---

* Psalm 144:16, *Douay Version*.

3. (a) Will it be a long time yet before God satisfies man's desire for peace and happiness? (b) Of what are worsening world conditions a proof?
4. (a) In God's new system, what causes for unhappiness will be things of the past? (b) How will God fulfill his promise of peace?

between nations, but among neighbors and in every household. Think what a grand blessing that could be to you! And how reassuring to know that the fulfillment of this heartwarming promise does not depend on men! It is God who will bring it about. How? By destroying the wicked and by educating his people in the ways of peace.—Proverbs 2:21, 22; Isaiah 54:13.

⁵ Among the many blessings that people will enjoy in the new system of God's making is good health. Even death, which brings much sorrow to all of us, will be no more. The Creator's promise is: "And [God] will wipe out every tear from their eyes, and death will be no more, neither will mourning nor outcry nor pain be any more. . . . Look! I am making all things new." (Revelation 21:4, 5)* That is something that no human ruler, no scientist, no doctor can do; but it is something that God will do. Is it reasonable that God's only purpose for man is that he spend twenty years growing up, perhaps another twenty or thirty years gaining knowledge and experience, and shortly thereafter begin to grow old, suffer from sickness and die? Why should man's life be so short when even a turtle may live to the age of two hundred years and a tree may live far longer? God made man to live, not to die. The Creator promises that soon it will be possible to enjoy life everlastingly, right here on earth. (Isaiah 25:8) With peace-loving neighbors, good health and satisfying activity to fill our lives, what a pleasure that will be!

---

* The Bible book of Revelation is called Apocalypse in the *Douay Version*.

5. (a) In the new system, what will happen to sickness and death? (b) What questions arise about man's present short life-span?

⁶ How can you be sure that this new system will come? How can you be sure it is not just a dream? You can be confident because Almighty God has promised it. The One who created and sustains the universe has given his guarantee that it will come. "God . . . cannot lie." (Titus 1:2) His word never goes unfulfilled.—Joshua 23:14.

⁷ These thrilling truths are found in God's Word, the Bible, the Holy Scriptures. There is no other source of information available to man that explains in a truly satisfying way the reason for what has happened on earth and God's purpose for mankind. While men were used to write the Bible, they did so under the direction of God's powerful active force or holy spirit, so that "all Scripture is inspired of God." (2 Timothy 3:16) Just as an invisible radio beam can carry information to you, so God's invisible active force directed the writers of the Bible to put down what he wanted mankind to know. That is why one of those writers, the apostle Paul, could say: "When you received God's word, which you heard from us, you accepted it, not as the word of men, but, just as it truthfully is, as the word of God." —1 Thessalonians 2:13; see also 2 Peter 1:20, 21.

WORLDWIDE CHANGE NEAR

⁸ God's Word of truth tells us very clearly that we are fast nearing a worldwide change. It shows us that our time is the one Jesus Christ had in mind when he foretold the end of this wicked system. Jesus foretold many things that his future followers should watch for so they would know

6. How can we be sure that this new system will come?
7. Even though men were used to write the Bible, why can we truthfully view it as "the word of God"?
8. What are some events that Jesus said would mark the last days of this wicked system?

when the end was near. He said that the last days
of this wicked system would be marked by such
things as world wars, food shortages, increasing
lawlessness and a growing loss of faith in God.
(Matthew 24:3-12) He said there would be
"anguish of nations, not knowing the way out."
(Luke 21:25) We have seen the fulfillment of
these prophecies in our lifetime.

[9] Many men who study world events are convinced that a great change is definitely in the
making. The famous writer Walter Lippmann said:
"For us all the world is disorderly and dangerous,
ungoverned and apparently ungovernable. Everywhere there is great anxiety and bewilderment."
He added that all this "marks, I believe, the his-
toric fact that we are living through the closing
chapters of the established and traditional way
of life."* Also, as reported back in 1960, a former
United States Secretary of State, Dean Acheson,
declared that our time is "a period of unequaled
instability, unequaled violence." And he warned:
"I know enough of what is going on to assure you
that, in fifteen years from today, this world is
going to be too dangerous to live in."†

[10] All the many things foretold in God's Word
of truth indicate that the time for world change
is upon us right now! What we see going on
throughout the world today in fulfillment of Bible
prophecy shows that our time is the one that will
see the destruction of this entire wicked system.
Present-day governments will be removed to make

---

* *Newsweek,* October 9, 1967, p. 21.
† *U.S. News & World Report,* June 13, 1960, pp. 116, 119.

9. Give an example or two of what men who study world
events say about our time.
10. (a) How do we know that world change is very near?
(b) For what does the coming world change mean destruction?

way for the rule of all the earth by God's government. (Daniel 2:44; Luke 21:31, 32) Nothing can stop this change, because God has purposed it.

TRUTH THAT LEADS TO ETERNAL LIFE

[11] The coming world change will affect every person on the face of the earth, including you. If you love life and want to live, you should hasten to take in accurate knowledge of God, his purposes and his requirements. That is what God wants you to do, for it is his will that "all sorts of men should be saved and come to an accurate knowledge of truth." (1 Timothy 2:4) Accurate knowledge from God's Word of truth will enable honest-hearted persons to survive the end of the present wicked system. (Zephaniah 2:3)* It will also reveal the way to eternal life in God's grand new system. Jesus Christ said in prayer to God: "This means everlasting life, their taking in knowledge of you, the only true God, and of the one whom you sent forth, Jesus Christ."—John 17:3; see also John 4:14.

[12] How encouraging it is to know that soon we will see the end of all the world's troubles! How thrilling it is to know that we have the hope of shortly entering a new system where we can forever enjoy life to the full! This should give every one of us strong reasons for wanting to learn the truth from the Bible. By seeking this truth we begin to lay "a fine foundation for the future, in order [to] get a firm hold on the real life," "eternal life" in God's new system of things.—1 Timothy 6:19; *AV*.

---

* Sophonias 2:3, *Douay Version*.

11. (a) Can we escape the effects of the coming world change? (b) So, if we want to live, what must we do, according to 1 Timothy 2:4 and John 17:3?
12. What strong reasons do we have for wanting to learn the truth from the Bible?

CHAPTER 2

Why It Is Wise to Examine Your Religion

WE HAVE good reason to think seriously about our standing with God. Why? Because the evidence proves that God will soon destroy the wicked and establish his righteous new system. So we need to ask: "Am I worshiping God in the way that he approves?" It is not any man, but God, who is the judge of what pleases him. To get God's viewpoint, we need to go to the Bible. There he plainly tells us the course to follow if we want to gain eternal life. (Proverbs 3:1, 2) If we take to heart what he says and apply it in our lives, it will result in marvelous blessings for us, both now and in the ages to come.

² When we examine what the Bible says on this matter, what do we find? Does it teach that the hundreds of millions of persons who practice religion in so many different ways are all pleasing to God? Does it show that all religion is good? To enable us to know how he views the matter, God had this plain statement recorded in his Word: "Broad and spacious is the road leading off into destruction, and many are the ones going in

1. (a) Since God will soon destroy this system of things, what question do we need to ask about our worship? (b) If we want to follow the course God approves, to what book will we go?
2. What statement in the Bible shows that not all religions are pleasing to God?

11

through it; whereas narrow is the gate and cramped the road leading off into life, and few are the ones finding it." (Matthew 7:13, 14) How clearly those words answer our questions! They show that many people are not worshiping God in a way that pleases him. Only a few are on the road leading to life.

[3] Probably you find yourself readily agreeing with the fact that much religion is not approved by God. No doubt there are many things done in the name of religion that you do not approve. For example, if you look around in the churches and observe persons who live immoral lives but who make a pretense at being righteous, you know that something is wrong. (2 Timothy 3:4, 5) And when you read in the newspaper that some clergymen are publicly approving of sex relations between unmarried persons and that they are saying that homosexuality is all right under certain conditions, you are well aware that this is not what God says. You may remember that God destroyed the ancient cities of Sodom and Gomorrah. And why? Because they practiced such things! So you know that God is not going to approve of a religion that tells people it is all right to act like that. —Jude 7.

[4] However, you have no doubt heard people say: "It doesn't matter what you believe, as long as you lead a clean moral life and deal kindly with your neighbors." But is that all there is to worshiping God in an acceptable way? These things are necessary, but God requires more. Doctrines are

---

3. Are there things done in the name of religion of which you do not approve?
4. (a) Besides our being moral and kind, what else must we consider about our religion, in view of Jesus' words at John 4:23? (b) Why do we need to examine the doctrines that we have been taught?

also involved. The Bible informs us that "the true worshipers will worship the Father with spirit and truth." (John 4:23) If our worship is to be acceptable to God, it must be firmly rooted in God's Word of truth. Jesus reproved those persons who claimed to serve God but who relied heavily on the traditions of men in preference to God's Word. He applied to them God's own words from Isaiah 29:13, saying: "It is in vain that they keep worshiping me, because they teach commands of men as doctrines." (Matthew 15:9) Since we do not want our worship to be in vain, it is important for each one of us to examine his religion.

[5] We need to examine, not only what we personally believe, but also what is taught by any religious organization with which we may be associated. Are its teachings in full harmony with God's Word, or are they based on the traditions of men? If we are lovers of the truth, there is nothing to fear from such an examination. It should be the sincere desire of every one of us to learn what God's will is for us, and then to do it.—John 8:32.

[6] The mere fact that church members may have the Bible or that it is occasionally read to them from the pulpit does not of itself prove that all the things they are taught are in the Bible. It is good to have the Bible; each and every person should. But we must also know what it says and believe it. If a religion really accepts the Bible as God's Word, it is not going to use certain parts of it and reject other parts. "All Scripture is inspired of

---

5. Why should we examine, not only our personal beliefs, but also the teachings of any religious organization with which we may be associated?

6. (a) Does the fact that the Bible is occasionally used in a church prove that all the church doctrines are from the Bible? (b) Why must religion approved by God agree in all details with the Bible?

God and beneficial for teaching, for reproving, for setting things straight." (2 Timothy 3:16) Since this is so, the religion that is approved by God must agree in all its details with the Bible.

⁷ The man who wants to please God must be sincere. But sincerity alone does not make one's religion approved in God's eyes. The apostle Paul was moved by God's spirit to write concerning certain ones in his day: "I bear them witness that they have a zeal for God; but not according to accurate knowledge; for, because of not knowing the righteousness of God but seeking to establish their own, they did not subject themselves to the righteousness of God." (Romans 10:2, 3) As a result, their sincerity was misdirected. Their problem was that they were looking in the wrong direction for instruction. They held onto the Jewish religious system, which had rejected God's Son and so was itself rejected by God.—Acts 2:36, 40; Proverbs 14:12.

⁸ What, then, of the religions that take the name of Christ and profess to accept him as their Lord? Does their preaching in his name guarantee that they meet with God's approval? In view of the scriptures already considered, perhaps you have concluded that it does not. If so, then on this matter you agree with Jesus Christ, the one whom God has appointed as heavenly judge; because he warns us, saying: "Not everyone saying to me, 'Lord, Lord,' will enter into the kingdom of the heavens, but the one doing the will of my Father who is in the heavens will. Many will say to me in that day, 'Lord, Lord, did we not prophesy in

7. As shown by the apostle Paul, does the sincerity of the worshipers in itself indicate that their religion is approved by God?
8. How did Jesus Christ show that not all religion that claims to be Christian meets with God's approval?

your name . . . ?' And yet then I will confess to them: I never knew you! Get away from me, you workers of lawlessness."—Matthew 7:21-23.

[9] Knowledge of the Bible and of God's will is essential for God's approval. But, as Jesus said, it is the *doing* of that will that counts. One must have works that are consistent with what one has learned. (James 2:26) To please God, then, one's religion must be in full harmony with the Bible and be applied in every activity of life.—Luke 6: 46-49.

[10] Jesus said that you could recognize whether a man practices the true religion by his "fruits," that is, the things he does. (Matthew 7:20) In the same way, we can recognize a religion by the kind of people it produces. True religion ought to produce better persons—better husbands and fathers, better wives and mothers. It should produce persons who are honest, who stand out among others because they do what is right. Is that not what you would expect of a religion that truly draws one close to God? God looks for these things too, and they determine whether a religion is approved of God or not.

[11] Certainly you do not want to be classed with those who are refused entry into the kingdom of God because of failure to do God's will. It will be to your benefit, then, to get well acquainted with the Bible. The book that you are now reading is designed to help you do that. Follow the course of those ancient Beroeans whom God's Word ap-

---

9. What besides Bible knowledge is needed for one's religion to be pleasing to God?
10. What fruitage will true religion bring about in the personal lives of those who practice it?
11. What course taken by people in ancient Beroea do we do well to follow?

proves because they "received the word with the greatest eagerness of mind, carefully examining the Scriptures daily as to whether these things were so."—Acts 17:11.

[12] As you examine God's Word, you will learn that your love for God will be put to the test. There may be individuals, perhaps even close friends or relatives, who will not approve of your examining the Scriptures. (1 Peter 4:4; Matthew 10:36, 37) They may try to discourage you. They may do this in all sincerity, because they do not know the marvelous truths found in the Bible. Perhaps you can help them. In other cases the opposition may come from persons who have no love for God. If this should occur, remember, having God's approval is far more important than having the approval of men. It is God, not man, who will give you eternal life if you love him above everyone and everything else.—Matthew 22:37-39.

[13] Always look to God for his help and guidance. Keep on praying, as did the psalmist: "O Jehovah, hear my prayer . . . Teach me to do your will, for you are my God." (Psalm 143:1, 10 [142:1, 10, *Dy*]) If you sincerely want to know and practice the religion that he approves, he will answer your prayer. And he will bring you into association with those who really do "worship the Father with spirit and truth."—John 4:23; see also Matthew 7:7, 8.

12. (a) How may our love for God be put to the test, perhaps by friends and relatives? (b) Whose approval should we always seek?
13. If we seek to do God's will, for what should we pray?

CHAPTER 3

Who Is God?

MAN'S need for God and his help has never been greater than now. Our lives depend upon knowing him. But, strangely enough, there is much confusion as to who he is, for today, as in the past, there are many gods worshiped in different lands. Yet the Bible makes clear that there is only one true God.—1 Corinthians 8:5, 6.

2 To distinguish himself from the many false gods, the true God has given himself a personal name. This sets him apart from all others. "Is not 'God' his name?" some may ask. No, for "God" is merely a title, just as "President," "King" and "Judge" are titles. God's personal name is made known to us through his Word, the Bible, and that name is JEHOVAH. In many translations of the Bible this name is found at Psalm 83:18, where we read (*AV*): "That men may know that thou, whose name alone is JEHOVAH, art the most high over all the earth." And in almost all translations the name is found at Revelation 19:1-6 as part of the expression "Alleluia" or "Hallelujah." This means "praise Jah" (a shortened form of Jehovah). *The Catholic Encyclopedia* (1910, Vol. VIII, p. 329) says of this Divine Name: "Jehovah, the proper name of God in the Old Testament."

---

1. Why is there much confusion as to who God is?
2. (a) Is "God" the personal name of the true God? (b) What is his personal name?

However, *The Jerusalem Bible,* a recent Catholic translation, regularly uses the name "Yahweh," as do a number of other translations. Why is that?

[3] In Hebrew, the language in which the first thirty-nine books of the Bible (*AV*) were written, God's name is represented thousands of times by four Hebrew letters, YHWH. In ancient times the Hebrew language was written without vowels, the reader supplying the vowels as he read the words. So, the problem is that today we have no way of knowing exactly which vowels the Hebrews used along with the consonants YHWH. Many scholars think the name was pronounced "Yahweh," but the form "Jehovah" has been in use for many centuries and is most widely known.

[4] Because there is uncertainty as to the exact pronunciation of God's personal name, some clergymen say you should not use it at all, but instead simply say "God" or "the Lord." However, they do not insist that you should not use the names "Jesus" and "Jeremiah." And yet these commonly used pronunciations are quite different from the Hebrew pronunciations "Yesh'ua" and "Yirm°iah'." The vital point is not what pronunciation you use for the Divine Name, whether "Yahweh," "Jehovah," or some other, as long as the pronunciation is common in your language. What is wrong is to *fail* to use that name. Why? Because those who do not use it could not be identified with the ones whom God takes out to be "a people *for his name.*" (Acts 15:14) We should not only know God's

3. (a) How is God's name represented in the Hebrew Scriptures? (b) Why is it not possible to know exactly how God's name was pronounced in Hebrew in ancient times?
4. (a) How are clergymen who say we should not use God's name because we do not know its exact pronunciation inconsistent? (b) What is far more important than how we pronounce God's name? (c) Why is it important to use God's name, in view of Acts 15:14?

name but honor it and praise it before others, as God's Son did when on earth.—Matthew 6:9; John 17:6, 26.

GOD'S QUALITIES AND WHY WE SHOULD WORSHIP HIM ALONE

⁵ What does the Bible itself tell us about God? It tells us that "God is a Spirit." (John 4:24) A spirit is not composed of flesh and blood, nor of other material substances that can be seen or felt by human senses. (1 Corinthians 15:44, 50) So, human eyes have never seen God. (John 1:18) He is far superior to anything our eyes behold. The majesty of the mountains, the brilliance of the sun, and even the glory of the starry heavens are nothing as compared to him.—Isaiah 40:25, 26.

⁶ No wonder that in the heavens the song is sung: "Great and wonderful are your works, Jehovah God, the Almighty. Righteous and true are your ways, King of eternity. Who will not really fear you, Jehovah, and glorify your name, because you alone are loyal?" (Revelation 15:3, 4) As the Creator of all things, Jehovah God, the "King of eternity," existed before all others. He is "from everlasting to everlasting," meaning that he had no beginning and will never have an end. —1 Timothy 1:17; Psalm 90:2, *AV* [89:2, *Dy*].

⁷ How right, then, that our worship should go only to him! As we consider his creative works, we too can say: "You are worthy, Jehovah, even our God, to receive the glory and the honor and the power, because you created all things, and because of your will they existed and were created."

---

5. Why has no human ever seen God?
6. (a) How does the Bible at Revelation 15:3, 4 describe God's qualities? (b) Did God have a beginning?
7. (a) According to Revelation 4:11, why is it right that our worship go only to Jehovah? (b) By means of what did God accomplish the creation of all things?

(Revelation 4:11) He accomplished the creation, not with tools such as men use, but by means of his holy spirit, which is his invisible active force. (Genesis 1:2; Psalm 104:30 [103:30, *Dy*]) It is that same holy spirit by which he later caused the Bible to be written so that we might know his will and purposes for men on earth.—2 Peter 1:21.

⁸ Since all things were created 'because of his will,' they all must serve God's purpose. Jehovah informed the first man and woman, Adam and Eve, of his purpose for them, and he held them accountable to act in harmony with it. Are we, too, accountable to God? Yes, because God is the Source of our life. This is true, not only because we have descended from that first human pair to whom God gave life, but also because our continued life each day depends on the sun, rain, air and food from which Jehovah continues to let us benefit. (Psalm 36:9 [35:10, *Dy*]; Matthew 5:45) To what extent, then, do we live our lives in harmony with God's purpose for us? We ought to think seriously about this, because our opportunity for eternal life is at stake.

⁹ Are we really to fear God? Yes, but with a healthy fear of rebelling against his will, because his will is *right*. In even ordinary things, do we not fear to take risks that could cause injury or loss of life? How much more so should we fear to displease "Jehovah God, the Almighty." Yet we can be glad that he is almighty, for "as regards Jehovah, his eyes are roving about through all the earth to show his strength in behalf of those whose heart is complete toward him." (2 Chronicles 16:

---

8. (a) Why are we accountable to God? (b) So, what question ought we to think about seriously?
9. (a) In what way should we fear God? (b) Why can we be glad that Jehovah is almighty?

9;* see also Isaiah 40:29-31.) And we may be sure that Jehovah always uses his power with a right purpose and for the good of those loving what is right. For "God is love."—1 John 4:8.

¹⁰ Jehovah, therefore, is not an oppressive God. "All his ways are justice." (Deuteronomy 32:4) True, he is "a God exacting exclusive devotion," but he is also "a God merciful and gracious, slow to anger and abundant in loving-kindness and truth." (Exodus 20:5; 34:6) "He himself well knows the formation of us, remembering that we are dust." (Psalm 103:14 [102:14, *Dy*]) We can be happy indeed to have such a just yet compassionate God as our Supreme Judge, Lawgiver and King.—Isaiah 33:22.

¹¹ With Jehovah there are "wisdom and mightiness; he has counsel and understanding." (Job 12:13) Evidence of his wisdom is seen in all his creative works, in both heaven and earth. We may well ask, then: "Why should anyone ever doubt God's wisdom?" The Bible shows that his requirements are for our good, with our everlasting welfare in view. It is true that there may be times when we, as humans having limited knowledge and experience, do not fully appreciate why a certain law stated by God is so important, or how it really works for our good. Yet our firm belief that God obviously knows far more than we do, that his experience is so much greater than ours, and that what he does is for our everlasting good, will move us to obey him with a willing heart.—Psalm 19:7-11 [18:8-12, *Dy*]; Micah 6:8.

* 2 Paralipomenon 16:9, *Dy*.

10. What qualities of Jehovah make us happy to have him as our God?
11. Even if we may not understand the reason for a certain law of God, what will move us to obey it?

IS GOD A "TRINITY"?

[12] Many religions of Christendom teach that God is a "Trinity," although the word "Trinity" does not appear in the Bible. The World Council of Churches recently said that all religions that are part of that Council should advocate the belief that there is "one God, Father, Son and Holy Spirit," that is, three persons in one God. Those teaching this doctrine admit that it is "a mystery." The Athanasian Creed, of about the eighth century of the Common Era, says that the Father, the Son and the Holy Ghost (Spirit) are all three of the same substance, all three are eternal (and hence had no beginning), and all three are almighty. So the creed reads that in the "Trinity none is afore or after other; none is greater or less than another."* Is that reasonable? More importantly, is it in agreement with the Bible?

[13] This doctrine was unknown to the Hebrew prophets and Christian apostles. The *New Catholic Encyclopedia* (1967 edition, Vol. XIV, p. 306) admits that "the doctrine of the Holy Trinity is not taught in the OT [Old Testament]." It also admits that the doctrine must be dated as from about three hundred and fifty years after the death of Jesus Christ. So the early Christians who were taught directly by Jesus Christ did not believe that God is a "Trinity."

[14] When Jesus was on earth he certainly was *not* equal to his Father, for he said there were

---

* *Cyclopædia of Biblical, Theological, and Ecclesiastical Literature*, by J. M'Clintock and J. Strong, Vol. II, p. 561.

12. (a) What do church creeds, such as the Athanasian Creed, teach about God? (b) What questions should we ask about this teaching?
13. According to the *New Catholic Encyclopedia*, did the Hebrew prophets and the first Christians believe in a "Trinity"?
14. How did Jesus show that he was not equal with his Father?

some things that neither he nor the angels knew but that only God knew. (Mark 13:32) Furthermore, he prayed to his Father for help when undergoing trial. (Luke 22:41, 42) Also, he himself said: "The Father is greater than I am." (John 14:28) Because of this, Jesus spoke of his Father as "my God" and as "the only true God."—John 20:17; 17:3.

[15] After Jesus' death, God raised him to life again and gave him glory greater than he had before. However, he was still not equal to his Father. How do we know? Because later the inspired Scriptures state that God is still "the head of the Christ." (1 Corinthians 11:3) The Bible also says that Jesus is to reign as God's appointed king until he has put all enemies under his feet, and that then shall "the Son also himself be subject unto him that put all things under him, that God may be all in all." (1 Corinthians 15:28, *AV*) Clearly, even since his resurrection Jesus Christ is not equal with his Father.

[16] But did not Jesus say on one occasion, "I and the Father are one"? (John 10:30) Yes, he did. However, that statement does not even suggest a "Trinity," since he spoke of only two as being one, not three. Jesus was surely not contradicting the scriptures we have already read. What he meant by this expression he himself made clear later when he prayed regarding his followers that "they may be one just as we are one." (John 17:22) Jesus and his Father are "one" in that Jesus is in full harmony with his Father. And he prayed that all his followers might likewise be in harmony

---

15. How do we know that Jesus was not equal with God even after he was raised from the dead?
16. (a) Does Jesus' statement, "I and the Father are one," teach a "Trinity"? (b) What did Jesus mean by that expression?

with his Father, with Jesus and with one another.

¹⁷ What about the statement at John 1:1 (*AV*), which refers to Jesus as "the Word," saying: "In the beginning was the Word, and the Word was with God, and the Word was God"? Does that not prove the "Trinity"? No. Notice, first of all, that only two persons are mentioned, not three. Also, in this same chapter, verse 2 says that the Word was "in the beginning *with* God," and verse 18 says that "no man hath seen God at any time," yet men have seen Jesus Christ. For these reasons, and in full harmony with the Greek text, some translations of verse 1 read: "The Word was with God, and the Word was divine," or was "a god," that is, the Word was a powerful godlike one. (*AT; NW*) So this portion of the Bible is in agreement with all the rest; it does not teach a "Trinity."*

¹⁸ As for the "Holy Spirit," the so-called "third Person of the Trinity," we have already seen that it is, not a person, but God's active force. (Judges 14:6) John the Baptist said that Jesus would baptize with holy spirit even as John had been baptizing with water. Water is not a person nor is holy spirit a person. (Matthew 3:11) What John foretold was fulfilled when God caused his Son Christ Jesus to pour out holy spirit on the apostles and disciples during the day of Pentecost 33 C.E., so that "they all became filled with holy spirit." Were they "filled" with a person? No, but they were filled with God's active force.—Acts 2:4, 33.

---

* Trinitarians have practically ceased to cite the words "the Father, the Word, and the Holy Ghost: and these three are one" that appear in some Bible versions at 1 John 5:7. Textual scholars agree that these words are a later spurious addition to the inspired text.

---

17. Why does the statement at John 1:1 not teach a "Trinity"?
18. How does the Bible account of what took place at Pentecost of 33 C.E. show that the holy spirit could not be a person?

[19] What, then, do the facts show as to the "Trinity"? Neither the word nor the idea is in God's Word, the Bible. The doctrine did not originate with God. But, you will be interested to know that, according to the book *Babylonian Life and History* (by Sir E. A. Wallis Budge, 1925 edition, pp. 146, 147), in ancient Babylon, the pagans did believe in such a thing; in fact, they worshiped more than one trinity of gods.

WORSHIPING GOD "WITH SPIRIT AND TRUTH"

[20] To love and respect a person, one needs to know him as he really is. To give God the exclusive devotion that he deserves, you need to study his Word and 'prove to yourself the good and acceptable and perfect will of God.' (Romans 12:2) The important thing is not how humans want to worship God, but how God wants to be worshiped.

[21] Religious ceremonies and "aids to devotion" may seem beautiful in the eyes of those who use them, but how does God view them? Surely you want to know, because you want to have God's approval. God's own Son tells us that "the true worshipers will worship the Father with spirit and truth." (John 4:23) Is the use of images, for example, worship "with spirit and truth"? Does it please God?

[22] At Exodus 20:4, 5, in one of the Ten Commandments, God himself says: "You shall not make yourself a carved image or any likeness of

19. (a) So, is the "Trinity" a Bible teaching? (b) In what ancient land did the pagans believe in trinities of gods?
20. According to Romans 12:2, what must we do to give God exclusive devotion?
21. In the words of God's own Son, how does God want to be worshiped?
22. (a) What does the Bible, at Exodus 20:4, 5, say about religious images? (b) What does God's Word say to show that the use of images as an "aid" to worship is no part of true worship?

anything . . . you shall not bow down to them or serve them." (The Catholic *Jerusalem Bible*) Some people regard a religious image simply as an "aid" to worshiping God because they can see and touch the image. But God inspired the apostle Paul to write: "We are walking by faith, not by sight." (2 Corinthians 5:7) God is very frank about the matter. He tells us that the use of images is no part of true worship, but that such images are "a falsehood." (Isaiah 44:14-20; Psalm 115:4-8 [113: 4-8, second set of numbers, *Dy*]) Even though one may say that the honor given to a religious image is less than that given to God, God himself says that he will not share any of his glory and praise with such images.—Isaiah 42:8.

²³ Lovingly, the apostle John warns us: "Guard yourselves from idols." (1 John 5:21) Why not look around your home and ask yourself whether you are doing this? (Deuteronomy 7:25) By bringing your life and way of worship into harmony with Jehovah's loving will you may gain his everlasting blessings.—1 Corinthians 10:14.

²⁴ Continue to learn of Jehovah's majesty and his loving purposes, and you will grow in love for him. Never let a day go by without thanking him for the good things that you enjoy because of his loving-kindness. As you learn more about him, impress upon your heart the importance of loyalty to him as the great God of the universe. By loving obedience to him, you will put yourself in the way that leads to eternal life.—Ephesians 4:23, 24; Psalm 104:33-35 [103:33-35, *Dy*].

---

23. As we look around our homes, what words of the apostle John should we keep in mind?
24. If we truly want to draw close to God, what should we do?

CHAPTER 4

Why We Grow Old and Die

EVERY normal person desires life with good
health. We seek relief from the pain and suffering that disease brings and we long for some
way to escape from the weakening effect old age
has on our bodies. It hurts us, too, when we see
those we love afflicted by these things. Because of
this, many persons ask, "Was all this part of God's
original purpose? When God created man, was it
his purpose that man should grow old, and become
deaf or blind? Did he mean for man's skin to
wrinkle with age, his heart to become diseased and
his other organs to break down? Really, did God
make man to die?"

² No, Jehovah God did not create man for such
a miserable future. The Bible tells us that Jehovah
provided a lovely garden home for the first human
pair, and he blessed them. Reviewing his creative
work, God rightly declared it "very good." (Genesis 1:28, 31) This means that Adam and Eve were
created perfect, without a defect in mind or body.
(Deuteronomy 32:4; Proverbs 10:22) They had
the prospect of living forever.

1. (a) What is the desire of normal persons respecting health
and life? (b) Because sickness and death are everywhere,
what questions are raised about God's purpose for man?
2. (a) Did God create man with any defect? (b) What prospect, then, did God give Adam and Eve?

[3] Interestingly, modern scientists know that the human body continually renews itself. And they say that, under the right conditions, it is capable of living forever. A Nobel Prize winner, Dr. Linus Pauling, explained that man's bodily tissues replace themselves and, theoretically, should continue to do so forever. Biochemist William Beck also observed: "I can see no reason why death, in the nature of things, need be inevitable." Yet, in spite of being so made, men continue to grow old and die. Why? God's Word the Bible gives us the satisfying answer.

RESULTS OF DISOBEDIENCE

[4] When Jehovah created Adam and Eve, they became the earthly part of God's great family, which already included a great number of spirit creatures in the heavens. God was the Father of the human pair, since he had given them life. The gift of life, however, was conditional; that is, it would continue to be theirs only as long as they met the condition of loving obedience to their heavenly Father. Obedience to law is necessary to continued peace and good order, so they had to recognize God as their Supreme Ruler. Did they know this? Yes, because Jehovah placed upon them a test that emphasized the seriousness of obedience. He said to Adam: "From every tree of the garden you may eat to satisfaction. But as for the tree of the knowledge of good and bad you must not eat from it, for in the day you eat from it you will positively die."—Genesis 2:16, 17.

[5] This test of obedience was not a difficult one.

3. What do scientists say about the life potential of humans?
4. What test did God place upon Adam and Eve, emphasizing the seriousness of obedience?
5. (a) Would the test of Adam and Eve's obedience put a hardship on them? (b) Why was the 'forbidden fruit' not sex relations?

They were not deprived of needed food, nor were they tested beyond their ability. However, their obedience would show that they appreciated their relationship with God. (1 John 5:3) Although some persons have the idea that the 'forbidden fruit' had to do with sex relations between the man and woman, this was not the case. God himself had already told them to "be fruitful and become many and fill the earth." (Genesis 1:28) When God commanded them not to eat the fruit of a certain tree it merely meant that God singled out one of the many fruit trees of Eden and commanded the human pair not to eat of its fruit.

[6] Why was the tree called "the tree of the knowledge of good and bad"? Because, as a result of God's command, its fruit symbolized God's right to decide for his creatures what is "good" and what is "bad" for them. So, for the human pair to take of this fruit would mean that they were turning their backs on their heavenly Father and rejecting his divine guidance and perfect will. While simple, the test involved much. It involved man's dependence on his Creator and man's recognition of divine authority. Remember, too, that Jesus Christ applied to imperfect humans the rule that "the person faithful in what is least is faithful also in much, and the person unrighteous in what is least is unrighteous also in much." (Luke 16:10) How much more did this apply to perfect creatures!

[7] Why did Eve break God's law and eat of the fruit? The idea did not begin with her but was

6. (a) Why was the tree called "the tree of the knowledge of good and bad"? (b) When Adam and Eve ate the fruit, what bad thing were they doing in regard to their heavenly Father? 7. (a) What did an invisible creature, speaking through a serpent, tell Eve about the tree's fruit? (b) What did Eve then do, and when her husband found out, what did he do?

presented to her by a spirit creature using a lowly serpent through which to speak. That spirit creature, identified in the Bible as Satan the Devil, is therefore called "the original serpent." (Revelation 12:9) The invisible creature speaking through the serpent openly denied the truth of God's command that Eve quoted. He represented the tree's fruit as being able to cause her to be like God, deciding for herself what was "good" and what was "bad." Eve then began to view the fruit as very desirable and she disobeyed God by eating of it. Adam, her husband and head, upon finding out what she had done, did not oppose her course but joined her in it.—Genesis 3:1-6; James 1:14, 15; 1 Corinthians 11:3.

⁸ By this lawless act they became guilty of sin, and so they brought upon themselves the penalty of sin. (1 John 3:4) In considering the rightness of God's decision we should not make the mistake of judging the

Adam deliberately violated God's plainly stated law

8. (a) By their lawless act, of what were Adam and Eve guilty? (b) Why should we not judge the seriousness of what Adam and Eve did by the way people view disobedience and stealing today?

seriousness of what Adam and Eve did by the way many people view things in our time. Today disobedience to parents is common, often going unpunished. Stealing also is common, and many think that, if what is stolen is small, the theft does not matter much. Rebellion and speaking against authority are likewise frequent today. But that does not make these things right! Much of the rotten fruitage we see today in the form of growing delinquency and crime is due to failure of parents and others in authority to correct matters at the start.—Proverbs 13:24; Ecclesiastes 8:11.

⁹ God was not going to encourage wrongdoing by a failure to enforce his own law. By their disobedience Adam and Eve showed a great lack of love for the One who had provided so wonderfully for them. They were guilty of stealing, because they took what their Creator said was not theirs. Still worse, they joined with God's enemy and, by their actions, called God a liar. Jehovah owed it to himself and to all his universal family to uphold the law. This he did. As a result of their deliberate sin the lawless couple were driven out of Eden to die.—Genesis 3:22-24.

¹⁰ The effect of sin upon them might be illustrated by what happens to a piece of fine machinery when it is not used properly, according to the maker's instructions. The machine will develop weaknesses and, in time, break down. Similarly, as a result of ignoring the instructions of their Maker, Adam and Eve lost their perfection. Their minds and bodies began to break down, and finally ceased to function, in death. That is what disobe-

9. (a) Considering what Adam and Eve really did, why did God owe it to himself and his universal family to uphold the law? (b) What penalty did the lawless couple suffer for their sin? 10. How can the effect of sin be illustrated with a piece of machinery, and to what did sin lead Adam and Eve?

dience and removal from God's favor meant for them. (Genesis 3:16-19) After Adam had used up the tremendous vitality of his once-perfect body, he died at the age of 930 years. This was within the symbolic "day" of one thousand years that God had set.—Genesis 5:5; 2 Peter 3:8.

EFFECT UPON OFFSPRING

[11] But, since we today did not disobey that law in Eden, why is it that we also get sick and die? It is for this reason: All of Adam's offspring were born after his disobedience. Thus his offspring inherited sin and death from him. All men inherit imperfection, because all come from Adam and Eve. As the Bible book of Job tells us: "Who can produce someone clean out of someone unclean? There is not one." (Job 14:4) Also, at Romans 5: 12 the Bible explains: "Through one man [Adam] sin entered into the world and death through sin, and thus death spread to all men." Just as a perfect piece of machinery cannot be produced from an imperfect mold, so Adam in his imperfection could not produce perfect children, free from sin. —Psalm 51:5 [50:7, *Dy*].

[12] The effect of Adam and Eve's sin upon their offspring can be compared with what often happens when people who ignore God's law and live immorally bring forth children. Such people may get diseased in the sex organs that God gave them to bring forth their children. The children of such "unclean" parents may be born physically or mentally damaged because of the sin of their parents. So, too, our first parents became "unclean," imperfect, subject to sickness, and finally death. They

11. How does the Bible explain why we today get sick and die?
12. How can the effect of Adam and Eve's sin be compared to what happens when persons who live immorally bring forth children?

could pass on to their offspring only what they themselves had: imperfection, with a future of sickness and death. That is why we all grow old and die, and why we so easily do what is wrong.

[13] However, it is one thing to make unintentional mistakes because of inherited sin, but entirely another matter deliberately to practice what one knows to be wrong. (1 John 5:16) If one is truly repentant over mistakes he makes because of inherited weaknesses, he can expect merciful forgiveness from God. (Proverbs 28:13) But he must be careful that, once he knows what is right, he does not deliberately choose to follow a course contrary to God's will. To do so would mean loss of God's favor and of life itself.—Deuteronomy 30:15-20; Hebrews 10:26, 27.

[14] Happily, Jehovah has made loving provision to save repentant ones from the bad effects of inherited sin and death. This grand relief will come through the ransom sacrifice of Jesus Christ. Concerning this provision the Bible says: "God sent forth his only-begotten Son into the world that we might gain life through him." (1 John 4:9) So, in God's due time, under the Kingdom rule of his Son, inherited human imperfection will gradually be taken away, and mankind will no longer feel the effects of Adam's sin. Why, even the death we inherited from Adam will no longer have power over us! (Revelation 21:3, 4) You can be one who will enjoy such blessings. How? By taking advantage of the provisions that Jehovah has made and proving your love for him by keeping his commandments.—Ecclesiastes 12:13.

---

13. Is there a difference between deliberate sin and unintentional sin? How so?
14. What provision has God made to save mankind from sin and death?

CHAPTER 5

Where Are the Dead?

PERHAPS you have experienced the empty feeling that comes with losing a loved one in death. On such occasions most persons feel not only sad but also very helpless. It is only natural to wonder: What happens to a person when he dies? Is he still conscious somewhere? Is there a real hope that the dead will live again? The Bible contains a comforting answer to these questions.

2 Simply stated, death is the opposite of life. In sentencing the first man Adam for his willful disobedience, God said: "You [will] return to the ground, for out of it you were taken. For dust you are and to dust you will return." (Genesis 3:19) Consider now: Where was Adam before God formed him from the dust and gave him life? Why, he simply did not exist. At his death Adam returned to the same lifeless, unconscious state. He went neither to a fiery hell nor to heavenly bliss, but died—as God said he would.—Genesis 2:17.

3 The Bible clearly teaches that the dead are unconscious and lifeless in the grave. Note what Ecclesiastes 9:5, 10 (*AV*) says regarding the condition of the dead: "For the living know that they shall die: but the dead know not any thing, neither have they any more a reward; for the memory of

1. What questions do people commonly ask about the dead?
2. What does the Bible say happened to the first man Adam at his death, and so what is death?
3. What does Ecclesiastes 9:5, 10 say about the condition of the dead, and what happens to man's thinking at death?

34

them is forgotten. Whatsoever thy hand findeth to do, do it with thy might; for there is no work, nor device, nor knowledge, nor wisdom, in the grave, whither thou goest." This means that the dead cannot do anything and cannot feel anything. Their thoughts have ceased, as the Bible states: "Put not your trust in princes, nor in the son of man, in whom there is no help. His breath goeth forth, he returneth to his earth; in that very day his thoughts perish."—Psalm 146:3, 4, *AV* [145: 2-4, *Dy*].

DOES MAN HAVE AN IMMORTAL SOUL?

⁴ But what about the soul? Is it not a part of man that separates from his body at death and goes on living? To answer this properly we need to determine what the soul is. You may be surprised to know that animals as well as men are called "souls" in the inspired Scriptures. For instance, Numbers 31:28 speaks of "one soul [Hebrew, *neph'esh*] out of five hundred, of humankind and of the herd and of the asses and of the flock." —See also Revelation 16:3, where the Greek word for "soul," *psykhé* appears.

⁵ What, then, is the soul? Let us see what the Creator's own written Word says about it. At Genesis 2:7 we read: "And Jehovah God proceeded to form the man out of dust from the ground and to blow into his nostrils the breath of life, and the man came to be a living soul."

⁶ Note, please, that after God started man breathing "the man *came to be a living soul*." Hence the man *was* a soul, just as a man who be-

4. What does Numbers 31:28 reveal about the word "soul"?
5. How does the Bible describe the soul?
6. What Bible facts about the human soul show that it could not be a shadowy thing that can exist apart from a person? So what is the human soul?

comes a doctor *is* a doctor. (1 Corinthians 15:45) Since the human soul is man himself, then it cannot be some shadowy thing that merely inhabits the body or that can exist apart from the person. In harmony with this fact, the Bible makes plain that the human soul possesses physical qualities. For example, the Bible speaks of the soul's desiring physical food, saying: "Your soul craves to eat meat." (Deuteronomy 12:20; see also Leviticus 17:12.) It says, too, that souls have blood traveling through their veins, for it speaks of "the blood of the souls of the poor innocents." (Jeremiah 2:34, *AV*) Yes, your soul is really *you,* with all your physical and mental qualities.—Proverbs 2:10.

⁷ What, then, of the texts that use such expressions as "my soul," or those that speak of a person's soul as though it is within him? These texts, of course, must harmonize with the scriptures already considered, for there can be no contradiction in God's Word. It becomes evident, then, that the word "soul" may be used in different senses. At times it refers to *one's own self as a soul.* So just as one says "myself" he also can say "my soul," meaning basically the same thing. Thus the psalmist wrote: "My soul has been sleepless from grief."—Psalm 119:28 [118:28, *Dy*].

⁸ "Soul" can also refer to *the life one enjoys as a living soul or person.* Now, we can say that someone *is* alive, meaning he is a live person. Or we can say that he *has* life, meaning he has life as a person. In the same way, man, according to the Bible, *is* a soul; but, as long as he is alive, he can be said to "*have* soul." So, just as we speak of

7. When the Bible uses the expression "my soul," to what is it referring?
8. (a) In what other way can the word "soul" be used? So can a live person be rightly said to "have soul"? (b) What Bible accounts speak of one's losing his life or soul?

one's losing his life, we can speak of his losing his soul. Jesus said: "For what is a man profited, if he shall gain the whole world, and lose his own soul?" (Matthew 16:26, *AV*) When Rachel had trouble in giving birth to Benjamin, her soul (or life as a soul) went out from her and she died. (Genesis 35:16-19) She ceased to be a living person and became a corpse. And when the prophet Elijah performed a miracle in connection with a dead child, the child's soul (or life as a soul) came back into him and "he came to life." He was again a living soul.—1 Kings 17:17-23.*

⁹ Since the soul is the person himself, what happens to a soul at death? The Bible is very clear in stating that the soul is subject to death, saying: "The soul that is sinning—it itself will die." (Ezekiel 18:4, 20) The apostle Peter quoted from the writings of Moses concerning Jesus, saying: "Indeed, any soul that does not listen to that Prophet will be completely destroyed from among the people." (Acts 3:23) Consistent with this basic truth, not once in any of its verses does the Bible say that either human or animal souls are immortal, deathless, cannot be destroyed or cannot perish. There are, however, dozens of scriptures that show that the soul can die or be killed. (Leviticus 23:30; James 5:20) Even of Jesus Christ the Bible says: "He poured out his soul to the very death." (Isaiah 53:12) We see, then, that the human soul is the person himself, and when the person dies, it is the human soul that dies.

¹⁰ Much of the misunderstanding about death

---

* 3 Kings 17:17-23, *Dy*.

9. (a) Does the Bible say that the human soul is deathless? (b) What scriptures show that the human soul can die?
10. Confusion about what two words has caused much of the misunderstanding about death?

has been due to the confusion in many persons' minds as to the meaning of "soul" and "spirit." The Bible shows they are not the same, as we shall see.

WHAT IS THE SPIRIT IN LIVING CREATURES?

[11] From Job 34:14, 15 we learn that there are two things that man (or any other conscious earthly creature) must have in order to be and stay alive: spirit and breath. There we read: "If he [God] sets his heart upon anyone, if that one's spirit [Hebrew, *ru'ahh*] and breath [Hebrew, *neshamah'*] he gathers to himself, all flesh will expire together, and earthling man himself will return to the very dust." We know that the first man was formed by God out of the "dust of the ground," that is, the elements taken from the soil. At the time of Adam's creation, God caused the billions of cells in his body to live, to have in them the force of life. This active life force is what is meant here by the word "spirit" (*ru'ahh*). But for the life force to continue in each of Adam's billions of cells, they needed oxygen, and this was to be provided by breathing. So, God next "breathed into his nostrils the breath [*neshamah'*] of life." Then Adam's lungs began to function and thereby sustain by breathing the life force in his body cells.—Genesis 2:7, *AV*.

[12] This was similar to the case of certain new-born babies. Although there is life in the baby when born, it sometimes does not begin to breathe right after birth. The doctor finds it necessary to spank the child to make it start breathing, for without breath the child would soon die. So, too, the life in Adam's body cells had to be sustained

11. (a) According to Job 34:14, 15, what two things must man have to stay alive? (b) Explain what each of these means.
12. Illustrate the "breath of life" by what can happen to a newborn baby.

by the breathing process in order for Adam to carry on the activities of a living person.

[13] Whereas the human soul is the living person himself, the spirit is simply the life force that enables that person to be alive. The spirit has no personality, nor can it do the things a person can do. It cannot think, speak, hear, see or feel. In that respect, it might be likened to the electric current of a car's battery. That current can ignite the fuel to make the engine produce power, cause the headlights to shine, sound the horn, or cause the car's radio to produce voices and music. But, without the engine, headlights, horn or radio, could that battery current do any of these things by itself? No, for it is merely the force that enables the equipment to perform and do such things.

[14] This spirit or life force is found in all living creatures, being passed on from parents to offspring at the time of conception. Thus, God told Noah that he would cause a flood of waters "to bring to ruin all flesh, in which the active force [*ru'ahh*, spirit] of life is," both of animals and men.—Genesis 6:17, *margin*, 1953 edition; see also 7:15, 22, *AV*, marginal reading.

[15] Because they all have this same life force or spirit, man and the animals die in a similar manner. For that reason, Ecclesiastes 3:19, 20 says: "There is an eventuality as respects the sons of mankind and an eventuality as respects the beast, and they have the same eventuality. As the one dies, so the other dies; and they all have but one spirit [*ru'ahh*] . . . All are going to one place.

13. (a) Does the spirit have personality? (b) Using the illustration of an automobile, to what can the spirit be compared?
14. Do animals have life force or spirit the same as man does?
15. How does Ecclesiastes 3:19, 20 show that both men and animals have this spirit or life force?

They have all come to be from the dust, and they are all returning to the dust."

[16] Since God is the Giver of life, his Word says that when a person dies "the dust returns to the earth just as it happened to be and the spirit itself returns to the true God who gave it." (Ecclesiastes 12:7) At death the life force eventually leaves all the body cells and the body begins to decay. All conscious thought and actions end. (Psalm 104: 29 [103:29, *Dy*]) How, then, does the spirit 'return to God who gave it'? Does the life force literally leave the earth and travel through space to God's presence? No, but it returns to God in the sense that now the future life prospects of the person rest entirely with God. Only God can restore the spirit, causing the person to live again.

[17] Some persons live in fear of the dead and make offerings to appease dead ancestors. But we can find comfort in knowing that, since the dead are unconscious, it is not possible for them to harm the living. And though one may have loved very much some person who died, God's Word shows that one cannot benefit the dead person by having religious acts or ceremonies performed for such one, perhaps at great expense to the survivors. (2 Samuel 12:21-23)* The knowledge of the true condition of the dead also protects us against the practice of trying to speak with the dead. The Bible warns that those who claim to speak with the dead are really getting in touch with demons, wicked spirits that falsely pretend to be the one who has died.—Deuteronomy 18:10-12.

---

* 2 Kings 12:21-23, *Dy*.

16. (a) In what way does the spirit leave the body at death? (b) How does it return to God?
17. (a) Can a dead person harm the living, or a living person benefit a dead person? (b) Our knowing the truth about the condition of the dead protects us from what demonic practice?

WHAT IS HELL?

[18] Many religious organizations teach that the wicked are tormented endlessly in a hellfire. But is this belief taught in God's Word? You may know the meaning that your own particular church organization gives to "hell," but have you ever investigated to see the meaning given it in the Scriptures? What is hell according to the Bible?

[19] In the Hebrew Scriptures of the Bible the word "hell" is translated from the Hebrew word *sheol'*. This word occurs 65 times in all. The King James Version of the Bible, however, translates *sheol'* 31 times as "hell," 31 times as "grave," and 3 times as "pit." The Catholic Douay Version of the Bible translates *sheol'* as "hell" 63 times and as "pit" once and as "death" once. In the Christian Greek Scriptures the word "hell" is sometimes translated from the Greek word *hádes*. Both the *King James* and *Douay* versions translate *hádes* as "hell" in each of its ten occurrences.

[20] Is hell a hot place? Do *sheol'* and *hádes* refer to some place where the wicked suffer after death? It is plain that they do not, for we have already seen that the dead are not conscious and therefore cannot suffer. The Bible does not contradict itself with regard to the condition of those in hell. This is proved by the fact that the Bible says that Jesus was in hell. (Acts 2:31, *AV, Dy*) When the apostle Peter stated this on the day of Pentecost, he clearly meant that Jesus had been in the grave, not in

18. What do many religious organizations teach about hell, and what questions arise concerning it?
19. (a) From what Hebrew word is the word "hell" translated? And how is this Hebrew word rendered in various Bible versions? (b) The word "hell" is sometimes translated from what Greek word?
20. (a) Why is hell not a place where people suffer? (b) Was Jesus in hell?

a place of fiery torment. (1 Corinthians 15:3, 4)
In saying this the apostle quoted from Psalm 16:10
[15:10, *Dy*]. Here the Hebrew word *sheol'* was
used, and at Acts 2:31 this word is translated by
the Greek word *hádes*. This shows that *sheol'* and
hádes refer to the same thing. The Bible "hell" is
actually mankind's grave.

²¹ As further proof of this, consider the case of
Job, a righteous servant of God who suffered
much. He prayed to God: "Who will grant me
this, that thou mayst protect me in hell [*sheol';*
the grave, *AV*], and hide me till thy wrath pass,
and appoint me a time when thou wilt remember
me?" (Job 14:13, *Dy*) How unreasonable to think
that Job desired protection in hell if it is a fiery-hot
place! Clearly, this "hell" is simply the grave, and
Job desired to go there so that his sufferings might
end. Good people as well as bad people go to the
Bible "hell," the common grave of all mankind.

RICH MAN AND LAZARUS

²² There is one place where *hádes* occurs, however, that has caused some persons to believe that
the Bible hell is a place of physical torment. That
is where Jesus spoke of the rich man and Lazarus,
and said that the rich man died, and in *hádes* experienced torment. (Luke 16:22-31) Why is the
use of *hádes* here so different from its use in other
places? Because Jesus was giving a parable or
illustration and was not speaking of a literal place
of torment. (Matthew 13:34) Consider: Is it reasonable or Scriptural to believe that a man suffers
torment simply because he is rich, wears good
clothing and has plenty to eat? Is it Scriptural to

21. (a) Did the righteous man Job believe hell to be a fiery-
hot place? (b) So what is the Bible hell?
22. How do we know that Jesus' words about the rich man and
Lazarus are an illustration?

believe that one is blessed with heavenly life just because he is a beggar? Consider this too: Is hell literally within speaking distance of heaven so that an actual conversation could be carried on? Also, if the rich man were in a literal burning lake, how could Abraham send Lazarus to cool his tongue with just a drop of water on the tip of his finger? What, then, was Jesus illustrating?

[23] In this illustration the rich man stood for the class of religious leaders who rejected and later killed Jesus. Lazarus pictured the common people who accepted God's Son. The Bible shows that death can be used as a *symbol*, representing a great change in one's life or course of action. (Compare Romans 6:2, 11-13; 7:4-6.) A death, or change from former conditions, happened when Jesus fed the Lazarus class spiritually, and they thus came into the favor of the greater Abraham, Jehovah God. At the same time, the false religious leaders "died" with respect to having God's favor. Being cast off, they suffered torments when Christ's followers after Pentecost forcefully exposed their evil works. (Acts 7:51-57) So this illustration does not teach that some dead persons are tormented in a literal fiery hell.

GEHENNA AND PURGATORY

[24] Perhaps someone may object and say that the Bible does speak of "hell fire." (Matthew 5:22, *AV*, *Dy*) True, some versions use this expression, but in such cases the original Greek word here used for "hell" is *Géenna,* and not *hádes.* Gehenna

---

23. What is the meaning of the illustration with regard to (a) the rich man? (b) Lazarus? (c) the death of each? (d) the torments of the rich man?
24. (a) When some Bible versions speak of "hell fire," from what original Greek word is the term "hell" translated? (b) How was Gehenna used when Jesus was on earth?

occurs twelve times in the Christian Greek Scriptures, and refers to the valley of Hinnom outside the walls of Jerusalem. When Jesus was on earth this valley was used as a huge garbage dump where fires were kept burning by adding brimstone (sulfur) to burn up the refuse. *Smith's Dictionary of the Bible,* Volume I, explains: "It became the common lay-stall [garbage dump] of the city, where the dead bodies of criminals, and the carcasses of animals, and every other kind of filth was cast."

[25] So when Jesus said that persons would be thrown into Gehenna for their bad deeds, what did he mean? Not that they would be tormented forever. Jesus used that valley (Gehenna) of fire and brimstone as a proper symbol of everlasting destruction. That is what his first-century listeners understood it to mean. The "lake of fire" mentioned in Revelation has a similar meaning, not conscious torment, but "second death," everlasting death or destruction. It is evident that this "lake" is a symbol, because death and hell (*hádes*) are thrown into it. Such things cannot literally be burned, but they can be done away with, or destroyed.—Revelation 20:14; 21:8.

[26] What, then, about purgatory? This is said to be a place where human souls are conscious and going through fiery purging after death. Since the Bible clearly shows that the dead are unconscious, how could God be tormenting anyone in such a place? (Psalm 146:4 [145:4, *Dy*]) Actually, neither the word "purgatory" nor the idea of a "purgatory" occurs in the Bible.

25. (a) Of what is Gehenna a proper symbol? (b) What terms in the Bible book of Revelation are a symbol of the same thing?
26. Does the Bible ever mention such a place as purgatory?

WILL THE DEAD LIVE AGAIN?

[27] The Bible teaching on the true condition of the dead relieves one's mind of much unnecessary fear and worry regarding those who have died. To know that such ones are not suffering helps us to appreciate far more God's love, and his justice. Yet, one may still wonder, If a man dies and simply goes to the grave, what hope is there for the dead? The Bible reveals that there is a wonderful hope, the hope of living again.

[28] During his earthly ministry Jesus Christ showed his power over death, actually bringing dead persons back to human life. (Luke 7:11-16; John 11:39-44) He thus provided a preview of what he will do on a grand scale in God's new system of things. The heartwarming prospect is that then hell, mankind's common grave, will be emptied of its unconscious dead. (Revelation 20:13) Some receive a resurrection to heavenly glory as spirit creatures, even as did Jesus Christ. (Romans 6:5) However, the vast majority of mankind will be brought back to enjoy life on a restored earthly paradise.—Acts 24:15; Luke 23:43.

[29] In God's new system the resurrected dead, if they carry out God's righteous laws, will never need to die again. (Isaiah 25:8) Certainly this grand provision for blessing mankind is reason for us to take in more knowledge of Jehovah and his Son, Jesus Christ. Doing so can lead to our eternal life and blessing.

---

27. What hope is there for the dead?
28. (a) Of what did Jesus' raising of persons from the dead provide a preview? (b) To what will most people be resurrected?
29. What should Jehovah's grand provisions for blessing mankind encourage us to do?

CHAPTER 6

Jesus Christ, the One Through Whom God Blesses Mankind

HOW loving the provision that Jehovah has made through his Son for blessing persons of all races and nations! He has promised deliverance from oppression, sin and death. What a glorious prospect! It is vital for us to appreciate, however, that these blessings will come to mankind only through Jesus Christ. For this reason, God inspired the apostle Peter to say of Jesus: "There is no salvation in anyone else, for there is not another name under heaven that has been given among men by which we must get saved." (Acts 4:12) By gaining accurate knowledge of this provision and by exercising faith in God's purpose in connection with Christ, you may put yourself in line for the grand blessings of eternal life.

² For thousands of years men of faith have awaited the fulfillment of this hope, and the promises of God gave them good reason for doing so. To the Hebrew family head Abraham, Jehovah made the promise that "all nations of the earth"

---

1. In what is it absolutely necessary for us to have faith if we are to receive the blessings of eternal life?
2. (a) What promise of blessing did God make to Abraham, and who did his "seed" prove to be? (b) To whom did the priesthood and sacrifices under the law of Moses point? (c) How does the Bible show who would be king of God's kingdom?

would be blessed through his "seed." That "seed" proved to be primarily Jesus Christ. (Genesis 22: 18; Galatians 3:14-16, 28, 29) God also provided for a priesthood and sacrifices under the Law given to Israel. These too pointed forward to Jesus. They directed attention to him as the great High Priest and to the sacrifice of his own human life as the means to take away sins forever and bring deliverance even from death. (Galatians 3: 24; Hebrews 9:11, 12; John 1:29) Furthermore, Jehovah foretold that the one through whom eternal peace would come to humankind would be of King David's family line and would become the king of God's kingdom, ruling over the entire earth. The angel Gabriel, in announcing Jesus' human birth, said: "This one will be great and will be called Son of the Most High; and Jehovah God will give him the throne of David his father." (Luke 1:32; see also Isaiah 9:6, 7; Daniel 7:13, 14.) Yes, the entire Word of God focuses attention on Jesus Christ as the one through whom Jehovah God will administer the blessings of eternal life to mankind.—Luke 2:25-32; Philippians 2:9-11.

PREHUMAN EXISTENCE

[3] Did you know that Jesus had a glorious existence long before he was born as a human here on earth? The Bible informs us that he is God's "firstborn" Son. This means that he was created before the other sons of God's family. He is also God's "only-begotten" Son, in that he is the only one directly created by Jehovah God; all other things came into existence through him as God's Chief Agent. Thus, before being born on earth as a male child he served in the heavens, where he was

---

3. (a) How is it that Jesus is God's "firstborn" Son? (b) Why does the Bible say Jesus is God's "only-begotten" Son?

known as "the Word," God's spokesman.—John
1:3, 10, 14; Colossians 1:15-17.

⁴ Jesus could therefore properly say: "Before
Abraham came into existence, I have been," and,
"I am the living bread that came down from heav-
en." (John 8:58; 6:51) Referring to the high position he had held in heaven, he prayed: "Father,
glorify me alongside yourself with the glory that
I had alongside you before the world was."—John
17:5.

HIS LIFE ON EARTH

⁵ In harmony with God's purpose for blessing
men of faith, the due time arrived for this heavenly Son to become a man on earth. This required a
miracle of God. Jehovah, by his holy spirit or
active force, transferred the life of Jesus from
heaven to the womb of a Jewish virgin girl named
Mary. Announcing this to Mary in advance, the
angel Gabriel said: "Holy spirit will come upon
you, and power of the Most High will overshadow
you. For that reason also what is born will be
called holy, God's Son." (Luke 1:35) It was well
within the power of the Creator to do this. Certainly the One who formed the first woman with
the ability to produce children could cause a
woman to conceive a child without a human
father, God himself being directly responsible for
the life of the child. This child, Jesus, was not
God, but God's Son. He was a perfect human, free
from the sin of Adam. How was that possible?
Because, as the angel said, the "power of the Most
High" was responsible; it even guided his growth
while in the womb of Mary.

4. What did Jesus say to bear witness to the fact that he had
lived in heaven before coming to earth?
5. (a) When God's time came for his Son to become a man on
earth, how did God bring this about? (b) How could the child
Jesus be born free from the sin of Adam?

[6] As foretold centuries before, Jesus was born in King David's city, Bethlehem of Judea. (Micah 5:2) He lived with his mother and his foster-father Joseph, working at the trade of carpentry until he was about thirty years of age. Then God's time came for him to do other work. So he went to John the Baptist to be baptized or dipped completely under the waters of the Jordan River. This showed that he was presenting himself to God to carry out the work that God had sent him to earth to do. By submitting to baptism Jesus set an example for all who exercise faith in him, and later he commanded that all who became his disciples should be baptized.—Matthew 28:19, 20.

[7] However, something else happened to Jesus at the Jordan. The heavens opened, God's spirit came upon him, and God himself spoke from heaven, saying: "This is my Son, the beloved, whom I have approved." (Matthew 3:16, 17) There was no mistake about it; this was the one whom all God's prophets had foretold! There at the Jordan, by means of holy spirit, Jesus was anointed by God to be the foretold great high priest, the king of God's kingdom, and to preach while here on earth. (Luke 4:16-21) There was work for him to do.

[8] For three and a half years he preached God's Word throughout the land, and he taught his disciples to do the same. (Luke 8:1) Though others in those days superstitiously avoided using the personal name of God, Jesus did not hold back from making it known. (John 17:26) He always

---

6. (a) As foretold in prophecy, where was Jesus born? (b) Why did Jesus get baptized?
7. What did God do at the time of Jesus' baptism?
8. Did Jesus hold back from using the personal name of God or from speaking the truth? So what should we do?

spoke the truth, whether it was popular or not. In what he did he provided an example that we should follow if we want to please God. But he also accomplished more than that.

RELIEF FROM SIN AND DEATH

⁹ Jesus knew that his coming to earth as a man was a direct part of God's arrangement for releasing humankind from sin and death. So he said: "The Son of man came . . . to give his soul a ransom in exchange for many." (Matthew 20:28) Exactly what does that mean? Well, a ransom is the price paid to obtain deliverance from captivity. In this case, Jesus' perfect human life offered in sacrifice was the price paid to obtain mankind's release from bondage to sin and death. (1 Peter 1:18, 19) Why was such a release needed?

¹⁰ This was because Adam, the forefather of us all, had sinned against God. Thus, Adam became imperfect and lost the right to life. As a willful violator of God's law, he came under its penalty of death. God had also established laws of heredity, which assure that we all receive physical characteristics and other traits from our parents. According to these laws, Adam could pass on to his offspring only what he himself had; so we received from him an inheritance of sin and death. (Romans 5:12) All mankind therefore has been dying in payment of the penalty of sin. How could this death penalty be lifted and the requirements of justice still be met?

¹¹ God did not weaken and compromise as to his

---

9. (a) According to Matthew 20:28, for what other reason did Jesus come to earth? (b) What is the ransom price that Jesus paid to release us from sin and death?
10. Why could we receive from Adam only an inheritance of sin and death?
11. In providing relief for Adam's offspring, how did God show due regard for law?

own laws. This would have merely encouraged further lawlessness by a bad example. Yet he did not turn his back on mankind and leave them without hope. While sticking to his laws, God lovingly provided relief, not for the willful sinner Adam, but for Adam's offspring, who, without any choice in the matter, suffered the effects of his wrong. God did this in harmony with a legal principle that he later included in the Mosaic law, namely, "soul will be for soul." (Deuteronomy 19: 21) Let us see how that principle applied in the ransom provided through Jesus.

[12] The "living soul" Adam, who forfeited life for mankind, was a perfect human. In exchange for what he lost, another human soul, equal to Adam, was needed, one who would offer his own perfect life as a sacrifice on behalf of mankind. (1 Corinthians 15:45) No offspring of Adam qualified for this, because all were born imperfect. As a result they all die because they are sinners, and they have no right to human life that they can sacrifice on behalf of others. (Psalm 49:7 [48:8, Dy]) So God sent his own Son to earth. Jesus was born as a human, because it was a human life that was required. But he was born without the aid of a human father, so that he would be perfect as Adam was. God alone was the Father of the human Jesus, as he had also been Adam's Father. (Luke 3:38) Thus Jesus was fully qualified to offer his life as a "corresponding ransom." —1 Timothy 2:6; Ephesians 1:7.

[13] On Nisan 14 of the year 33 C.E. Jesus' enemies put him to death on a torture stake. He could have resisted, but he did not. (Matthew 26:53, 54)

12. Who only could provide the ransom price for what Adam lost? So why did Jesus have to be born as a human?
13. Why did Jesus willingly lay down his life and not resist?

He willingly laid down his life in sacrifice for us. As his apostle Peter tells us: "He himself bore our sins in his own body upon the stake, in order that we might be done with sins and live to righteousness. And 'by his stripes you were healed.' "—1 Peter 2:24; see also Hebrews 2:9.

[14] That was indeed a marvelous expression of God's love for mankind! The Bible helps us to appreciate it, saying: "God loved the world so much that he gave his only-begotten Son, in order that everyone exercising faith in him might not be destroyed but have everlasting life." (John 3: 16) If you are a parent who has a dearly loved son, no doubt you can appreciate, at least to some extent, what that meant to God. It surely should warm our hearts toward him to realize that he cares for us so much.—1 John 4:9-11.

[15] Jehovah God did not leave his Son dead in the grave, but raised him to life on the third day. He was not given human life again, because that would have meant that he was taking back the ransom price. But he was "made alive in the spirit." (1 Peter 3:18) During a period of forty days after his resurrection he appeared visibly to his disciples a number of times, in materialized bodies, to prove that he really had been raised from the dead. Then, with the disciples looking on, he ascended heavenward and was caught out of sight in a cloud. He returned to heaven, there "to appear before the person of God for us" bearing the value of his ransom sacrifice as the great high priest. (Hebrews 9:12, 24) The requirements of

---

14. What does the Bible at John 3:16 tell us about God's love for mankind? So how should we respond?

15. (a) Was Jesus resurrected with a human body? (b) After his resurrection, why did Jesus appear visibly to his disciples? (c) Was it necessary for Jesus to return to heaven? Why?

divine justice had been met; relief was now available for mankind.

[16] Even now we may benefit greatly from the ransom. By exercising faith in it we can enjoy a clean standing before God and come under his loving care. (Revelation 7:9, 10, 13-15) When, due to imperfection, we commit a sin, we can freely seek forgiveness from God on the basis of the ransom, with confidence that he will hear us. (1 John 2:1, 2) Furthermore, the ransom has opened up the way for preservation through the end of this present wicked system of things. It makes possible the resurrection of the dead. And it provides the basis for gaining eternal life in God's new system of things, where it will be applied to mankind in order to wipe away all the effects of inherited sin.—1 Corinthians 15:25, 26; Revelation 7:17.

RULER OF THE KINGDOM OF GOD

[17] During his earthly ministry Jesus constantly directed attention to the kingdom of God. He taught his followers to pray: "Let your kingdom come. Let your will take place, as in heaven, also upon earth." And he urged them to "keep on, then, seeking first the kingdom." (Matthew 6:10, 33) Many of his parables drew attention to the Kingdom. He made it the theme of his preaching. (Matthew 9:35) By his miracles of healing and raising the dead, he showed on a small scale what will take place on earth under the kingdom of God. At that time sickness will come to an end, blind

---

16. (a) Explain how we benefit even now from the ransom provision. (b) As we consider the future, what does the ransom make possible for us and for the dead?
17. (a) To what did Jesus constantly draw attention, making it the theme of his preaching? (b) What did Jesus demonstrate by his miracles of healing and raising the dead?

eyes will be opened, deaf ears unstopped, and crippled arms and legs will be healed. What a blessing that will be!—Revelation 21:3, 4.

[18] Jesus himself is the one anointed by God as ruler of the Kingdom. However, when Jesus returned to heaven it was not the due time for him to exercise that kingly power. He must await his Father's appointed time. (Acts 2:34-36) Yet, he pointed forward to the time when he would return with Kingdom power, saying: "When the Son of man arrives in his glory, and all the angels with him, then he will sit down on his glorious throne. And all the nations will be gathered before him, and he will separate people one from another, just as a shepherd separates the sheep from the goats." (Matthew 25:31, 32) We are living in that time of separating now. Soon Christ on his heavenly throne will use his kingly authority to destroy the wicked and deliver sheeplike ones who will inherit the earthly realm of the Kingdom.—Matthew 25:34, 41, 46.

[19] By means of Jesus Christ blessings are available to all mankind, but we must exercise faith in him in order to receive them. (John 3:36) We must become his disciples and submit ourselves to him as our heavenly king. Will you do that? There are opposers who want to hinder you, but if you put your full trust in Jehovah you will without fail receive the blessings that God has in store for those who love him.—Psalm 62:7, 8 [61:8, 9, Dy].

---

18. (a) Did Jesus exercise kingly power as soon as he returned to heaven? Why? (b) According to Matthew 25:31, 32, what did Jesus say he would do when he returned with Kingdom power? 19. To enjoy blessings through Jesus Christ, what must we do?

CHAPTER 7

Are There Wicked Spirits?

JESUS CHRIST, who came to earth from the spirit realm, acknowledged the existence of wicked spirits. You may recall that he often spoke of the Devil, and that he called him "the father of the lie" and a "manslayer." (John 8:44) For our own protection in this time when lying and murder are on the increase, we do well to examine this subject.

[2] Many persons, of course, do not believe that there are wicked spirit creatures. Even some who claim to use the Bible say that Satan the Devil is only a quality of evil, not an invisible spirit person. But do the facts agree with their belief? What about Jesus Christ's own experience when the Devil tempted him? The Bible tells us that the Devil showed Jesus all the kingdoms of the world and said to him: "All these things I will give you if you fall down and do an act of worship to me." Jesus answered the Devil: "Go away, Satan! For it is written, 'It is Jehovah your God you must worship.'" Then the Devil left Jesus.—Matthew 4:1-11.

---

1. (a) Did Jesus believe that wicked spirits exist? (b) What did Jesus call the Devil?
2. (a) Contrary to what Jesus taught, what do some persons believe the Devil is? (b) What experience did Jesus have with the Devil?

³ During that experience, by whom was Jesus Christ tempted? By a real person? or by a mere quality of evil? If he was tempted by a mere quality of evil, in whom did this quality dwell? Was this evil in Jesus Christ? If so, then it could not be true that in him there was no sin. Yet the Bible, God's Word of truth, makes it very clear that Jesus was "guileless, undefiled, separated from the sinners." (Hebrews 7:26) The Bible also says: "He committed no sin, nor was deception found in his mouth." (1 Peter 2:22) So Jesus could not have been carrying on a conversation with "evil" in his own self. He was talking to a living spirit creature. Thus the Scriptures and sound reasoning make clear that Satan is a real, live person in the invisible spirit realm.—1 Peter 5:8.

A SELF-MADE DEVIL

⁴ But in what way did the Devil originate? Obviously, the God 'whose work is perfect' would not create someone wicked. (Deuteronomy 32:4) He would not create intelligent creatures with whom he could not associate. Such would be contrary to reason and God's love.—Psalm 5:4-6 [5:5-7, *Dy*].

⁵ So, the invisible spirit who later became the Devil must at one time have been perfect, without defect as a creation of God, just like all the other millions of angelic "sons of God." (Job 38:7) How, then, did he go bad? After the creation of the first man and woman, this particular spirit creature entered on a course of rebellion against God. He developed a desire to be worshiped and so enticed

3. (a) How does that experience show that the Devil could not be merely a quality of evil? (b) What, then, is Satan the Devil?
4. From what we know about God, why can we be certain that he would not create someone wicked?
5. (a) How did the spirit creature who became the Devil take a wrong course? (b) Was it a mere snake that put the idea of rebellion into the mind of Eve?

Adam and Eve to rebel against God. How did he do this? The Bible shows that a serpent spoke to Eve, telling her a lie. As a result she disobeyed God. Then she caused her husband to join her in revolt against God. But who actually put the idea of rebellion into Eve's mind? Was it a mere snake with no speech organs? No, there was someone behind the serpent making it appear as if it were talking. We know that some skilled humans can speak words with their lips nearly shut, making it appear as if a nearby animal or a dummy is talking. How much easier for a superhuman invisible person to do this! God made Balaam's ass speak. (Numbers 22:28) In Eden, Satan used the serpent. And so the Bible identifies the Devil, or Satan, as "the original serpent," hence the one who really introduced rebellion and wickedness into the universe.—Revelation 12:9; 2 Corinthians 11:3.

⁶ But, you may wonder, if this highly intelligent spirit really was perfect, how could he turn to wickedness when there was no one to tempt him? The Bible answers that it was by his thinking upon a wrong idea. (James 1:14, 15) There is nothing wrong in itself with seeing the possibilities in a certain situation. For example, a person in someone else's home may see money lying on a table. The possibility of his taking that money and putting it into his pocket is there. But, since that would be stealing, he should not even consider it. Or, if the idea does come into his mind, he ought to dismiss it. But if he keeps the idea in his mind and allows it to grow, then wrong desire develops. Soon this may move him to commit an act of wickedness.

---

6. How could a perfect creature turn to wickedness?

⁷ So, too, with the perfect spirit creature. The possibility was there of his using the human pair for his own purpose rather than carrying out what God wanted. As a free moral agent, he not only considered it but also failed to dismiss it from his mind, and it led him to sin. Just as a formerly honest man can make himself a thief by stealing, so this spirit creature made himself Satan by acting as a *resister* of God; and he made himself the Devil by becoming a *slanderer* of God, because that is what those names mean.

⁸ Of course, someone may say, "Might it not have been simply a mistake that he made? Could he not have apologized and so ended the matter there?" In answer, we need to keep in mind that a perfect individual is different from us. When he uses his free will, the choice that he makes is not due to weakness or imperfection. Imperfect people often make mistakes due to inherited weakness. They can admit their mistakes, apologize and change their course. But when a perfect creature chooses to do wrong, he does it deliberately and he does not later turn back to doing good. This was the case with the one who made himself the Devil.

OTHER SPIRIT CREATURES
MAKE THEMSELVES DEMONS

⁹ The Devil was not the only spirit creature to turn to disobedience and wickedness. God had created a great number of holy angels, millions of them. Daniel 7:10 reveals a portion of them as being 100,000,000. The Bible record at Genesis 6: 1-5 explains that before the flood of Noah's day

---

7. (a) So how did this spirit creature become wicked? (b) Who, then, made Satan the Devil?
8. Why was it not just a mistake that Satan made?
9. How did others of God's holy angels make themselves demons?

some of these spirit "sons of God" materialized as men, that is, they left their place in heaven as spirit creatures and clothed themselves with fleshly bodies. And why? To enjoy human passions by marrying the good-looking daughters of men. This was an act of disobedience to God, and the Bible associates it with the actions of the people of Sodom and Gomorrah who 'went after flesh for unnatural use.' (Jude 6, 7) So, too, it was against their heavenly nature for angels to come down and seek human flesh with which to have sex relations. Their course brought bad results, including a freakish offspring, "mighty ones" called Nephilim. By their rebellious action, those spirit sons of God turned themselves into demons and put themselves on the side of the Devil, who is the "ruler of the demons."—Matthew 9:34.

[10] When the global flood of Noah's day destroyed all the wicked humans, the unfaithful angels dissolved their fleshly bodies and returned to the spirit realm. But they were not allowed to become part of God's organization of holy angels again. Instead, they were confined in a debased condition of spiritual darkness. (2 Peter 2:4) Since the Flood, God has not permitted these demonic angels to materialize in the flesh as they did before then. Yet they can still exercise dangerous power over men and women. In fact, with the help of these demons Satan is "misleading the entire inhabited earth." (Revelation 12:9) The great increase in wrongdoing that we see all over the earth today should alert us to the need to be on guard against being misled by them.

10. (a) When the flood of Noah's day came, what happened to the disobedient angels who had married the daughters of men? (b) To what should the increase in wrongdoing in our day alert us?

THE DEVIL IS THE "RULER OF THIS WORLD"

[11] Three times in the Bible book of John we read that the Lord Jesus Christ called the Devil "the ruler of this world." (John 12:31; 14:30; 16:11) At 2 Corinthians 4:4 he is referred to as "the god of this system of things." Does this mean, then, that all the nations of the earth are under the control of Satan the Devil? The Bible answers: "The whole world is lying in the power of the wicked one." (1 John 5:19) Thus the Devil, as "ruler of the world," exercises great influence on men, overreaching them and even controlling political governments.—Revelation 16:13, 14.

[12] If you will open your Bible to Revelation 12:9, you will see that the Devil is described as "the great dragon." In the next chapter, verses 1 and 2, we are told that this dragon, the Devil, gave power and a throne and great authority to what is symbolically called a "wild beast" out of the sea. What is this symbolic "wild beast"? Well, over what does Satan hold authority? What did he offer to Jesus Christ? "All the kingdoms of the inhabited earth." (Luke 4:5-8) Jesus quickly rejected that offer, but he did not deny that the Devil ruled over the political kingdoms of the earth. In harmony with this, Revelation 13:7 says concerning the symbolic "wild beast," that "authority was given it over every tribe and people and tongue and nation." Further, with what did the prophet Daniel identify certain beasts? With "kingdoms,"

---

11. What position does Satan hold with regard to all nations?
12. (a) According to Revelation 13:1, 2, to what does the Devil give power and authority? (b) How does the Devil's offer to Jesus help us to identify the "wild beast"? (c) Since the account about the "wild beast" of Revelation 13:1, 2 and the one about the beasts of Daniel's vision both refer to the same kinds of animals, what must the "wild beast" represent?

or political governments. (Daniel 7:2-7, 17, 23) That the symbolic beasts of Daniel's vision and the "wild beast" of Revelation have a similar meaning is seen from the fact that both accounts refer to the same kinds of creatures: a lion, a bear, a leopard and a ten-horned beast. (Revelation 13:1, 2) So the "wild beast" represents the Devil's entire political organization that has exercised beastlike rule over the earth throughout the centuries until now. No wonder Jesus Christ said: "My kingdom is no part of this world." And no wonder that his followers would be no part of the world either, that is, they would avoid getting involved in its affairs.—John 18:36; 17:14-16.

KEEP FREE FROM EVERY FORM OF SPIRITISM

[13] One of the ways that wicked spirits mislead men and women is through spiritism. What is spiritism? It is getting in touch with wicked spirit creatures, being misled by them either directly or through a human or other medium. The Bible warns us to keep from every practice associated with spiritism, because spiritism brings a person under the influence of the demons.—Galatians 5:19-21; Revelation 21:8.

[14] God condemns every kind of spiritism. The Bible tells us what some of these disapproved things are: divination, magic, looking for omens, sorcery, binding others with a spell (hypnotism, black magic, and so forth), consulting a spirit medium or a fortune-teller and inquiring of the dead. (Deuteronomy 18:10-12; Isaiah 8:19) All of this is demonism, and those who turn to such

---

13. What is spiritism, and why does the Bible warn us to keep free from it?
14. What are some practices associated with spiritism, and how does God view those who turn to such practices?

practices make themselves enemies of God.—Leviticus 19:31; 1 Chronicles 10:13, 14.*

[15] Divination is one of the common forms of spiritism. It is the effort to obtain knowledge of the unknown or of the future by means of omens or demon power. (Acts 16:16) Many are the ways divination is practiced today, such as by divining rods, pendulums, crystal-ball gazing, Ouija boards, ESP, examining the lines of one's hand (palmistry), studying the flight of certain birds, looking for omens in one's dreams and in other incidents in one's life and then trying to relate these to the future. There is also divination by the stars, commonly called astrology. This originated in ancient Babylon, as did various forms of the magical arts. The Bible shows that all who use divination sin against God.—1 Samuel 15:22, 23.†

[16] One of the common ways in which wicked spirits mislead people is by talking to them, either through a spirit medium or by a "voice" from the invisible realm. The "voice" pretends to be a departed relative or a good spirit; but this is falsehood! The voice is actually a wicked spirit speaking! What should you do if such a "voice" speaks to you? Well, what did Jesus Christ do when the ruler of the wicked spirits spoke to him? Jesus rejected the Devil's suggestions, saying: "Go away, Satan!" (Matthew 4:10) You can do that too. Also, you can call on Jehovah for aid, praying aloud and using his name. Follow this wise course, and do not give ear to such voices from the

---

* 1 Paralipomenon 10:13, 14, *Dy*.

† 1 Kings 15:22, 23, *Dy*.

15. (a) What is divination, and what are some of the ways that people engage in it today? (b) Where did astrology and magic begin?
16. What should we do if we ever hear a "voice" from the invisible realm speak to us?

invisible realm.—Proverbs 18:10; James 4:7.

[17] But what if one has been dabbling in some of the spiritistic religions or sciences and now wants to break free from spiritism? Well, what did many of the early Christians at Ephesus do when they wanted to get free from the magical arts? The Bible tells us that, after accepting the "word of Jehovah" preached by the apostle Paul, they "brought their books together and burned them up before everybody," even though they were worth 50,000 pieces of silver! (Acts 19:19, 20) Their example of destroying objects related to spiritistic practices is the wise one to follow.

[18] Do not be deceived by the increasing interest in mystic and occult matters. Wicked spirit creatures are promoting such spiritism. But these wicked spirit forces, including the Devil, will eventually be destroyed. (Matthew 25:41) If you want eternal life you need to stay free from their influence by avoiding every kind of spiritism.

THE DEVIL PROMOTES FALSE RELIGION

[19] It should not surprise us that the Devil and his demons have many ways of misleading mankind, spiritism being just one of these. What, then, is the foremost means by which the Devil, "the father of the lie," turns mankind away from God? (John 8:44) It is by means of false religion! False religion is worship that is built on falsehoods and that is in conflict with God's Word of truth, the Bible. That is one reason why the Bible points out that if a person worships in a way that is not in

---

17. How can one break free of spiritism today by following the example of the early Christians at Ephesus?
18. (a) What will happen to all wicked spirits? (b) In view of this, what must we do if we want eternal life?
19. (a) What is the chief means by which the Devil turns mankind away from God? (b) What is false religion? (c) If one practices false religion, to whom is one really giving service?

harmony with God's Word, he is in reality serving the demons, because he is acting in harmony with what they want and in conflict with God.—Deuteronomy 32:16, 17; 1 Corinthians 10:20.

²⁰ Although false religions may appear respectable, we should realize that the Devil is like many modern-day underworld or crime leaders who hide behind a front of respectability. What more subtle way could there be for him to deceive people and get them to serve him than by using a religious front that has an outward appearance of righteousness? That the Devil would mislead people by religion that outwardly claims to serve God is shown in the Bible. (Matthew 7:22, 23) In fact, the Christian apostle Paul said that "Satan himself keeps transforming himself into an angel of light" and "his ministers also keep transforming themselves into ministers of righteousness."—2 Corinthians 11:14, 15.

²¹ So Jesus Christ was not imagining something when he called the Devil "the ruler of this world." (John 12:31) There are indeed wicked spirits misleading "the entire inhabited earth." But only a "short period of time" remains before the Devil and his wicked angels are to be put out of operation. (Revelation 12:9, 12) Meantime, keep free from every form of spiritism and break free from religion that may appear respectable but is really based on falsehood. You cannot hold to spiritism or any other religious falsehood and get eternal life in God's new system of things, because it is only the truth that leads to eternal life.—Ephesians 6:12, 16.

20. Like crime leaders, how does the Devil deceive people?
21. (a) What does the Bible show as to the time left for the wicked spirits? (b) Why should a person break free from spiritism and all other false religion?

CHAPTER 8

Why Has God Permitted Wickedness Until Our Day?

THROUGHOUT all of man's history there has been much wickedness. And today, no matter where you look in the world, there is bloodshed, crime, hatred and immorality. All too often it is the innocent, decent people who suffer from the wicked acts of others. They may be victims of violence, perhaps losing their homes, loved ones or even their own lives. You may or may not have experienced such things personally. Even if you have not, you likely have gone through things that have caused mental suffering, experiences such as injustice, unkindness, being cheated or deceived.

² Why has God permitted such wickedness until our day? There are a number of reasons, but to understand those reasons properly we need to examine the issues raised at the time of the first rebellion. You have likely read the account of this in the Bible in the third chapter of Genesis. Let us consider, then, the real meaning of these events.

³ Briefly, this is what occurred: Jehovah told man that his life depended upon obedience to his

1. What is mankind's experience regarding wickedness?
2. The reasons why God has permitted wickedness have to do with questions raised at what time?
3. Briefly relate what took place at the time of man's fall into sin.

Creator, and that disobedience would result in death. (Genesis 2:17) God's adversary, Satan, contradicted this clear statement. He told Adam's wife that the human pair could disobey and still, "You positively will not die." He further claimed that such disobedience would actually improve matters for them, causing their eyes to be opened, and that they would "be like God, knowing good and bad." (Genesis 3:4, 5) Now, what was involved in this rebellious action of Satan?

THE ISSUES AT STAKE

⁴ A number of issues or vital questions were raised. First, Satan called into question *the truthfulness of God*. In effect, he called God a liar, and that with regard to a matter of life and death. Second, he questioned *man's dependence on his Creator for continued life and happiness*. He claimed that neither man's life nor his ability to govern his affairs with success depended upon obedience to Jehovah. He argued that man could act independently of his Creator and be like God, deciding for himself what is right or wrong, good or bad. Third, by arguing against God's stated law, he in effect claimed that *God's way of ruling* is wrong and not for the good of his creatures and in this way he even challenged *God's right to rule*.

⁵ But Satan's action raised still another question, as is shown later in the Bible in the book of Job, chapters 1 and 2. There, in connection with a man named Job, it is shown that Satan called into question *the faithfulness and loyalty to Jehovah God of all creatures*. In so many words, Satan made the claim that those who serve God do so, not be-

4. Name some of the issues raised by the Devil's rebellion.
5. As shown in the Bible book of Job, what other question was raised by Satan?

cause they love God and his righteous rule, but only for selfish reasons, such as the material blessings God gives them. He claimed that, if such reasons were taken away, then even a man like Job would turn away from God. (Job 1:6-11; 2:4, 5) Yes, Satan's rebellion in Eden called into question the loyalty of all God's creatures in heaven and on earth. If put to the test, would they prove their love for their heavenly Father and show that they preferred his rule to that of any other?

GOD'S WAY OF SETTLING THE ISSUES

⁶ Note, please, that Satan did not raise any question as to God's strength. He did not challenge Jehovah to use his might to destroy him as an opposer. But he did challenge God's right to rule and the rightness of his way of ruling. Also, he questioned the loyalty of God's creatures. So it was a *moral* issue that had to be settled.

⁷ Satan's false charges against God may be illustrated, to a certain extent, in a human way. Suppose a man having a large family is accused by one of his neighbors of many false things about the way he manages his household. Suppose the neighbor also says that the family members have no real love for their father but only stay with him to obtain the food and material things he gives them. How might the father of the family answer such charges? If he simply used violence against the accuser, this would not answer the charges. Instead, it might suggest that they were true. But what a fine answer it would be if he permitted his own family to be his witnesses to show that their father was indeed a just and loving family head

6. Did Satan raise a question as to God's strength? So what kind of issue had to be settled?
7. Relate an illustration that shows how such a moral issue might be settled.

and that they were happy to live with him because they loved him! Thus he would be completely vindicated.—Proverbs 27:11; Isaiah 43:10.

⁸ This illustrates in certain respects what God has done. Moreover, he has allowed sufficient time —now almost 6,000 years—for the issue to be settled beyond all doubt. He has allowed this time, not only to permit his faithful creatures to prove their devotion to him and his rule, but also to demonstrate that any other kind of rule results only in bad. (Proverbs 1:30-33; Isaiah 59:4, 8) By rebelling against Jehovah God, Satan set himself up as a rival ruler. And, by taking the course Satan recommended, the first human pair declared themselves independent of Jehovah's rule and came under Satan's control. (Genesis 3:6; Romans 6:16) By God's letting both Satan and man go to the limit in their efforts to act and rule independently of their Creator, their total failure to produce good government, with real benefits for all mankind, would be made evident beyond all future denial. Meanwhile Jehovah would have those on earth who love him proclaim his name and purposes for the enlightenment of all who love and seek what is right.

⁹ So, the situation is much like that involving a Pharaoh of Egypt who took a course similar to that of Satan the Devil in opposing Jehovah God, and to whom Jehovah said: "By now I could have thrust my hand out that I might strike you and your people with pestilence and that you might be effaced from the earth. But, in fact, for this cause have I kept you in existence, for the sake of

8. What has been demonstrated by God's allowing enough time for the issue to be settled beyond all doubt?
9. What did God say to a Pharaoh of Egypt that is similar to the case of Satan the Devil?

showing you my power and in order to have my name declared in all the earth."—Exodus 9:15, 16.

WHAT HAVE THE RESULTS SHOWN?

[10] The Bible shows that Satan has made use of the time to build up an organization in heaven and earth over which he rules. The extent of his control of the earth is indicated by the fact that he could offer Jesus all the kingdoms of the world in exchange for Jesus' worship. (Matthew 4:8, 9) That is why Satan is called "the ruler of this world." (John 16:11) What has this meant for mankind, and what has been the result of man's course of independence from God and his rule?

[11] History testifies to the fact that this has not brought peace, contentment and eternal life to mankind. It has brought the opposite: thousands of years of pain, suffering and death. The record of history and the dreadful state of affairs in the world today are proof that man has not succeeded in governing without God. Man has tried all kinds of government, but he still lacks security and enduring happiness. True, there has been progress in a materialistic way. But is it really progress when men send rockets to the moon, and yet cannot live together in peace on earth? What good is it for them to build homes equipped with every convenience, only to have families torn apart by divorce and delinquency? Are wars, riots in the streets, destruction of life and property and widespread lawlessness something of which to be proud? Not at all! But they are the fruitage of rule that ignores God. Truly, as Ecclesiastes 8:9 says, "man has dominated man to his injury."

---

10. How has Satan used the time allowed by God with regard to both heaven and earth?
11. What has been the sad result of man's course of independence from God and his rule?

¹² So God's long permission of wickedness has proved beyond doubt that man's attempt to 'play God' is a miserable failure. (Psalm 127:1 [126:1, *Dy*]) As a prominent editor said: "The more we search for an alibi, the more we discover that unhappiness on earth is man-made. Our key weakness is that we have not solved the problem of self-government."* The inspired Bible writer Jeremiah rightly said: "I well know, O Jehovah, that to earthling man his way does not belong. It does not belong to man who is walking even to direct his step. Correct me, O Jehovah."—Jeremiah 10:23, 24; see also Proverbs 16:25.

¹³ Satan's influence over earth's affairs has brought disunity, wickedness and death, and his rule has been by means of deceit, force and selfishness. He has proved himself unfit to be the ruler of anything. So Jehovah is now fully justified in destroying this debased rebel along with all who have shared in his wicked deeds. (Romans 16:20) But what about the loyalty of God's creatures to Jehovah's loving rule and Satan's claim that *all* would turn away if put to the test?

¹⁴ Jehovah God knew that "love never fails" and he knew that some of mankind would serve him willingly, out of love, and not because they were being bribed or forced. (1 Corinthians 13:8) Many thousands have done this throughout the centuries. Job was one of these. Even though Satan

---

* David Lawrence, *U.S. News & World Report*, Sept. 25, 1967, p. 128.

12. (a) What did a prominent editor say about the cause of unhappiness on earth? (b) According to the prophet Jeremiah, can man safely direct his own step?
13. Since Satan's rule has proved a failure, what is God now fully justified in doing?
14. (a) Out of what fine motive have some of mankind served God willingly? (b) By Job's keeping his integrity to God despite pressure from Satan, what did Job prove the Devil to be?

brought terrific pressure against him and stripped him of his belongings, children and health, Job still declared: "Until I expire I shall not take away my integrity." (Job 27:5) Job proved Satan a liar.

[15] As we have seen, the perfect man Jesus resisted all of Satan's temptations and bribes. Further, when whipped by soldier guards and nailed to a cruel torture stake to die, Jesus held fast his loyalty to God. (1 Peter 2:23) This proved that perfect Adam could have done the same if he had wanted to, and that God was not unrighteous in requiring full obedience from man. (2 Thessalonians 1:4, 5) By his loyalty to Jehovah, Jesus gave the finest answer to Satan's false challenge.

[16] But Satan, his mind being twisted by selfishness and pride, has refused to slow down in his insane course. Although it has long since been proved that he was wrong and is a liar, he continues to persecute lovers of God. (Revelation 12: 17) Since Jesus' death many thousands of Christians have served Jehovah God because they loved him and wanted his loving rule over them. And right now, hundreds of thousands proclaim their loyalty to Jehovah as ruler. (Revelation 7:9, 10) Their faithful keeping of Jehovah's Word and their respect for his law have enabled them to live in contentment, in spite of all opposition from Satan. The unity, love and integrity displayed by God's servants throughout the centuries provide a mountain of evidence that Jehovah's way of ruling in love is the only right way, that man can

---

15. (a) How did Jesus answer Satan's false challenge against Jehovah? (b) Could perfect Adam have proved full loyalty to God?

16. (a) Though fully proved a liar, why does Satan still continue to persecute lovers of God? (b) Of what is the loyalty of God's faithful servants convincing evidence?

stay loyal to him under the most severe test, and that Satan is the most monstrous liar of all time.

HOW LONG WILL THE TEST CONTINUE?

[17] Jehovah has permitted wickedness until our day in order to settle all the issues raised by Satan. But he will not permit wickedness to continue indefinitely. He has set a definite time when he will bring it to an end. The Bible writer Daniel referred to this long ago when he wrote: "The end is yet for the time appointed."—Daniel 11:27.

[18] Nearly six thousand years from Adam's day to ours may seem a long time when viewed from the standpoint of humans who live about seventy years. But since God set the time limit, it is good to appreciate his view of the matter. The prophet Moses, at Psalm 90:4 [89:4, *Dy*], says of him: "A thousand years are in your eyes but as yesterday when it is past." A year is a long time to a child of five, but to a man of sixty it is comparatively short. Likewise, to Jehovah, who lives for eternity, a thousand years is like a day.—2 Peter 3:8.

[19] This set time during which wickedness has been permitted has been no injustice to us. Why, if God had immediately crushed the life out of all the rebels in Eden, we would never even have been born! We would never have had the opportunity for eternal life in his new system. So the fact that Jehovah did not cut short his long-suffering at some earlier time has given us opportunity to live now, and eternally in the future. (2 Peter 3:9, 15)

---

17. Will God permit wickedness indefinitely, and how does the Bible book of Daniel answer that question?
18. Although a time period of nearly 6,000 years seems long to man, does it seem long to God? So how does God view a thousand years?
19. Why has God's permission of wickedness been no injustice to us?

Also, God has used this time to provide for man's redemption through Christ.—Galatians 4:4, 5.

[20] In addition, God has used the time to select and prepare from among mankind "vessels of mercy." These are the ones who will make up the righteous government over those who will live forever on earth in the new system. What blessings this heavenly kingdom means for mankind! During the time that God has been preparing the "vessels of mercy," he has shown much long-suffering. He has tolerated the wicked, the "vessels of wrath." He has held off their destruction. Why? The Bible clearly answers: "In order that he might make known the riches of his glory upon vessels of mercy." (Romans 9:22-24) To God's heavenly kingdom will go the glory of vindicating God's name and destroying the wicked, the "vessels of wrath." Also, by his allowing wickedness to continue for a time, facets of God's personality are manifested that would not ordinarily be seen: his mercy and long-suffering. These enrich our appreciation of the Creator and our own personalities, as we imitate him.—Ephesians 5:1.

[21] There has also been another real benefit in God's permitting wickedness as long as he has. If at any time in the future anyone should call into question God's way of doing things, it would not be necessary again for him to grant that one time to try out some other way. The record of six thousand years of failure by Satan, his demons, and men who have tried to run affairs independent of God has supplied sufficient answer. No one can rightly claim: 'They did not get a chance,' or say,

20. How does the Bible at Romans 9:22-24 explain why God has permitted wickedness?
21. What other benefit has come by God's permitting wickedness to run its set time?

'If only they had more time.' The permitted time
has been enough to prove that the way of rebellion against the Creator has been absolutely
disastrous! So God will be fully justified in swiftly
crushing any rebel that threatens the future peace
of the universe.—Psalm 145:20 [144:20, *Dy*].

²² There is only a short time left before Jehovah
will destroy this wicked system of things. This
remaining time gives us the opportunity to take
sides with him and 'make his heart rejoice.' (Proverbs 27:11) If we willingly submit to his rulership,
he will bless us with eternal life in his new system.
The choice of accepting or rejecting is set before
each one of us.—Deuteronomy 30:19, 20.

²³ Obedience to God is not really difficult. If we
appreciate that Jehovah's wisdom is much greater
than ours, and that whatever he does is for our
good because he is a God of love, then we will obey
him in everything. Whatever Jehovah's will is, we
will want to do it, whether in times of crisis
or in the everyday things of life. That is the way
loyal servants of God have always felt. (Daniel
3:16-18; Psalm 119:33-37 [118:33-37, *Dy*]) In the
first century some of these said to a high court:
"We must obey God as ruler rather than men."
(Acts 5:29) Today, Jehovah is using his loyal
servants to declare his name and purposes in all
the earth. (Matthew 24:14) When that is done to
his satisfaction, then he will show Satan his almighty power by crushing him and all other rebels,
bringing an end to this wicked system. Thus, Jehovah will clear the universe of wickedness and pave
the way for his righteous new system.

22. How much longer will Jehovah permit wickedness, and
what opportunity does the remaining time give us?
23. (a) How should we view obedience to God? (b) After
God's loyal servants have done the work of declaring his name
and purposes in all the earth, what will Jehovah do?

CHAPTER 9

The Reason Why a "Little Flock" Goes to Heaven

WHILE Jesus Christ was yet with his followers here on earth, he spoke to them about heavenly life. He told them that he was going to prepare a place for them and that, in time, they would be there with him. (John 14:1-3) Millions of persons have set their hearts on such heavenly life. To them it has represented a prospect of relief from the troubles of this life. But do you know why God has arranged for some persons to go to heaven? Do you know what they will do there?

2 During his earthly ministry Jesus said much about the "kingdom of God." He taught his followers to pray that, by means of the Kingdom, God's will would be done here on earth. Thus, the earth would become a delightful home for mankind. But the kingdom, or government itself, would be that of God in heaven, and for this reason Jesus often referred to it as the "kingdom of the heavens." (Matthew 5:20; 6:9, 10) This helps us to understand what he meant when he said: "Have no fear, little flock, because your Father has ap-

---

1. (a) When Jesus was on earth, what did he tell his followers about heavenly life? (b) Why do many persons want to go to heaven?
2. (a) What is the kingdom of God, and where is it located? (b) So, when Jesus said that the "little flock" would inherit "the kingdom," what did that mean?

proved of giving you the kingdom." (Luke 12:32) Yes, God would give this "little flock" a share in the heavenly government over all mankind.

[3] At Revelation 20:6 we read concerning those who would be resurrected to heavenly life: "They will be priests of God and of the Christ, and will rule as kings with him for the thousand years." Jesus Christ is the principal king and the high priest, and these faithful ones taken from the earth serve with him.—Revelation 5:9, 10.

[4] Why are they chosen from the earth for such a work? Because it was here at this earth that Jehovah's rulership was challenged. It was here that the faithfulness of men to God could be put to the test under opposition from the Devil. It was here that Jesus proved his full loyalty to God under test and gave his life as a ransom for mankind. So it was from this earth that Jehovah arranged to take a "little flock" of persons to be associated with his Son in the heavenly kingdom. They are persons who show full faith in God's provision for salvation through Christ. They are ones whose lives prove the Devil a liar when he charged that men serve God only for selfish advantage. Jehovah has marvelously purposed to use them for his glory.—Ephesians 1:9-12.

[5] As kings and priests under the direction of Jesus Christ, they will serve from their heavenly positions in carrying out Jehovah's will toward mankind. How wonderful it will be to have as rulers those who have proved faithful to God!

3. What does Revelation 20:6 say that those resurrected to heavenly life will do there?
4. Why is it fitting that those whom God arranges to be in the heavenly kingdom are taken from this earth?
5. (a) Why is it a loving arrangement of God to put in office those who have experienced the problems common to mankind? (b) What blessings will earth's inhabitants enjoy when these heavenly priests apply the benefits of Christ's ransom sacrifice?

(Revelation 20:4) And how loving of God to put in office those who have experienced the problems common to humankind! Surely, they, like Christ, will deal in an understanding way with their subjects. (Hebrews 2:17, 18) What a blessing it will be to the inhabitants of earth as these heavenly priests apply to them the benefits of Christ's ransom sacrifice, healing them spiritually, mentally and physically until they reach perfection!—Revelation 21:2-4.

HOW MANY GO TO HEAVEN?

[6] Those who are called by God to share in such heavenly service are few in number. As Jesus said, they are a "little flock." Years after his return to heaven, Jesus made known the exact number in a vision to the apostle John, who wrote: "I saw, and, look! the Lamb standing upon the Mount Zion, and with him a hundred and forty-four thousand . . . who have been bought from the earth." (Revelation 14:1, 3) The "Lamb" referred to here is, of course, Jesus Christ; and this "Mount Zion" is not on earth, but in heaven where Jesus is. (John 1:29; Hebrews 12:22) So the 144,000 are persons who die on earth as humans and are resurrected to heavenly life as spirit creatures, as Jesus was. (Romans 6:5) When compared with the thousands of millions of persons who live on earth, they are, indeed, a "little flock."

[7] However, the "little flock" who go to heaven are not the only ones who receive salvation. As we have seen, they will have happy earthly subjects. Jesus referred to these as his "other sheep," of whom "a great crowd" are even now serving God faithfully.—John 10:16; Revelation 7:9, 15.

6. How many make up the "little flock"?
7. (a) Are the 144,000 the only ones to receive salvation? (b) By what term did Jesus refer to those who will live on earth?

HOW ONE KNOWS WHETHER HE IS OF
THE "LITTLE FLOCK"

⁸ Members of the "little flock" know that God has called them to heavenly life. How? By means of the operation of God's spirit, which implants and cultivates in them the hope of heavenly life. The apostle Paul, as one of the "little flock," wrote: "The spirit itself bears witness with our spirit that we are God's children. If, then, we are children, we are also heirs: heirs indeed of God, but joint heirs with Christ, provided we suffer together that we may also be glorified together." (Romans 8:16, 17) The operation of God's spirit changes the entire outlook of such a person, so that his thoughts and prayers are centered upon serving God with the heavenly hope in view. Being with Christ in heaven is more important to him than any earthly ties.

⁹ No doubt you have thought about this matter, and perhaps you have wondered whether you are one who will receive heavenly life. Before one can properly analyze his situation, he needs an understanding of what the Bible teaches on this matter. Why? Because God's holy spirit that bears witness that one has been called to heavenly glory is the same spirit that directed the writing of the Bible. With this in mind, let us examine the situation.

¹⁰ In the past did you believe that all good persons go to heaven? If so, and if you endeavored to live a good life, you may well have expected to be included among them. You may also have hoped in this way to be reunited with your loved

8. How does one who has been called to heaven know that?
9. Before one can analyze his situation with regard to heavenly life, what is needed?
10. (a) What belief may have caused one to expect to go to heaven? (b) What Bible truths are not known by those who think that all good people go to heaven?

ones whom you had lost in death. But when you had that expectation, did you know that the Bible says that such faithful servants of God as King David and John the Baptist did not go to heaven? (Acts 2:29, 34; Matthew 11:11) At that time did you know that only 144,000 chosen from among mankind over the past nineteen centuries would gain heavenly life? And did you know then that the Bible holds out hope of eternal life under righteous conditions here on earth for all others who would become faithful servants of God? —Psalm 37:10, 11, 29 [36:10, 11, 29, *Dy*].

[11] When you were then thinking about heavenly life for yourself, did you believe in the immortality of the human soul? Then, understandably, you may have hoped that your soul would go to heaven. But if you had such a hope it was not because God's spirit was bearing witness to you. To the contrary, as you now know, God's inspired Word says that the human soul dies and goes out of existence. So those who die must depend on God to resurrect them to whatever place he wills for them.—Ezekiel ·18:4; 1 Corinthians 15:35-38.

[12] In this matter, then, we must look to the Scriptures for guidance and not let emotions, or a background of unscriptural beliefs, confuse our thinking. Those who receive heavenly life are not persons who choose it for themselves; God is the one who does the choosing. (2 Thessalonians 2:13, 14) They are called on to leave behind close family members and friends and all earthly things for the privilege of sharing as assistant kings and underpriests with Christ and as part of his

11. Because of what false teaching as to the soul do many persons think that they will go to heaven?
12. (a) Who does the choosing of persons who will receive heavenly life? (b) To what hope is God principally pointing persons today?

"bride." (Revelation 21:2) That is what God has set before them, and they show deep appreciation for it. But it is not necessary to be of that heavenly group to gain relief from the troubles of this life. God loves his earthly "other sheep" too. He promises that he is going to make this earth a paradise, where pain and sorrow will be no more. The facts show that it is principally to such an earthly hope of life that God has been pointing persons in recent years.

[13] However, each year, on the anniversary of Christ's death, the few remaining members of the "little flock" yet on earth keep the Memorial of Christ's death. As Jesus directed, they partake of unleavened bread and red wine, which are symbols representing the flesh and blood that Jesus gave for mankind. Jesus said to those whom he instructed to partake of these emblems that he was making with them 'a covenant for a kingdom'; so those who are not heirs of the heavenly kingdom do not partake of the emblems. (Luke 22:19, 20, 29) Nevertheless, those who look forward to earthly life are present each year in large numbers as observers at the Lord's evening meal. As one who is keenly interested in life under the heavenly kingdom, you too should be in attendance.

THE RETURN OF CHRIST

[14] On the evening before his death Jesus Christ promised eleven faithful members of the "little flock" that he would come again, saying: "I am going my way to prepare a place for you. . . . I am coming again and will receive you home to myself, that where I am you also may be."—John 14:2, 3.

---

13. (a) Who properly partake of the bread and wine at the annual Memorial of Christ's death? (b) Who else are present?
14. What promise did Jesus make about coming again?

[15] Will this be a visible, physical return? Some may point out that Revelation 1:7 says: "Look! He is coming with the clouds, and every eye will see him." Does this mean that they will see him literally with their physical eyes? The Bible speaks not only of seeing with our physical eyes, but of seeing in the sense that we understand or discern. Jesus showed that the religious Pharisees of his day were blind although they said, "We see." They were spiritually blind. (John 9:39-41; Isaiah 43:8) It is in such a sense of spiritual seeing that Revelation 1:7 is to be understood. "Every eye" is made to "see" him because, even though they may refuse to show faith now, when Christ executes the wicked, they will know what is happening because they have been told in advance. However, that Jesus would not visibly return he himself made clear, saying: "A little longer and the world will behold me no more, but you will behold me, because I live and you will live." (John 14:19) Mankind in general would behold him no more because he was going to return to heaven. But the "little flock" would behold him because he was going to take them to be with him there.

[16] So Christ's return does not mean that he returns as a man to live on earth. Rather, it means that he takes up his kingly rule toward the earth and that he resurrects his "little flock" from the dead to their reward in the heavens. There they share in carrying out the loving purpose of God by means of his kingdom. You are living in the time when you, too, can experience blessings from that Kingdom rule.—Revelation 11:15-18.

---

15. (a) What does Revelation 1:7 say about Christ's return, and is this to be understood in a visible sense? (b) How do we know that mankind in general would not behold Christ at his return?
16. What, then, does Christ's return mean?

CHAPTER 10

God's Kingdom Comes to Power in the Midst of Its Enemies

FOR thousands of years men of faith have lived in eager expectation of the day when God's kingdom would begin its rule. They have felt keenly the need for God to take a direct hand in earth's affairs. Does this mean that God has not been King during the centuries past? No, for Jehovah has always been the Supreme Ruler of the universe. (Jeremiah 10:10) But here at the earth his rulership has been challenged. And, as we have already seen, for sound reasons and with a loving purpose in view, God has allowed human governments under the influence of Satan to rule for a fixed period of time.

² Jehovah promised, however, that at the end of that time he would take direct action against all rebels and opposers of his rule. And he would bring the earth and its inhabitants completely under his rule again. How? By the Kingdom, a new heavenly government under his Son Christ Jesus. So the coming of that kingdom to power means that great changes are near at hand. It means that Jehovah God has given to his Son

---

1. (a) To what have men of faith long looked forward? (b) Has not God always been King?
2. What is God's kingdom, and to whom does he give the ruling power?

"rulership and dignity and kingdom, that the peoples, national groups and languages should all serve even him."—Daniel 7:13, 14.

³ That event has already taken place in heaven. Kingdom authority has already been given to Jehovah's Son. Does that sound strange to you? It might, especially in view of the terrible conditions afflicting mankind. But, really, it is because of these very conditions that we can be certain that this is true. Why is this?

⁴ This is so because the coming to power of Jehovah's kingdom is not welcomed by all creatures. Not everyone wants to live under a government that insists on righteousness. (Luke 19:11-14) For this reason, Jehovah long ago recorded in his Word that when he 'begins ruling as king' toward the earth 'the nations would become wrathful.' (Revelation 11:17, 18) He foretold that, at the time of empowering his Son to act, it would be necessary for him to say: "Go subduing in the midst of your enemies."—Psalm 110:2 [109:2, Dy].

⁵ Christ Jesus would then oust Satan from heaven, the seat of government, hurling him down to the vicinity of the earth, in preparation for putting him completely out of action. In the heavens the grand announcement would then be made: "Now have come to pass the salvation and the power and the kingdom of our God and the authority of his Christ." But for the earth, what? "Woe . . . , because the Devil has come down to you,

3. Why may some at first find it strange to think that God's kingdom has already come to power?
4. (a) Why do not all creatures welcome God's kingdom? (b) So what was it foretold that God would say to his Son when granting him power to act as king?
5. What action was then to take place in heaven, and with what result for the earth?

having great anger, knowing he has a short period of time." (Revelation 12:5, 7-10, 12) Full control of earth by God's kingdom must soon follow! However, the start of the rule by God's kingdom does not mean immediate peace and righteousness on earth. To the contrary, it triggers a period of unprecedented trouble for earth's inhabitants.

[6] Realizing this, we can better understand the meaning of what Jesus told his followers about his second presence. They had asked him: "Tell us, When will these things be, and what will be the sign of your presence and of the conclusion of the system of things?" (Matthew 24:3) Jesus then described, for their benefit and ours, what would take place on earth when he would begin to rule in heaven. In this way, although the events in heaven would be invisible to human eyes, there would be visible proof that Christ was at last on the throne, taking action as king. It would be proof that the wicked system of things that has oppressed mankind for centuries had entered its "last days." (2 Timothy 3:1) Although it was foretold that there would be ridiculers that would try to belittle the facts, yet the evidence would be clear. —2 Peter 3:3, 4.

[7] As we consider the evidence together, it is important to realize that Jesus did not say that any one event, such as threat of war or a terrible earthquake, would be the proof that "the end" was at hand. (Matthew 24:6) Rather, he said: "Note the fig tree and all the other trees: When

6. (a) What question did Jesus' followers ask him about his second presence? (b) Why would a visible "sign" be needed? (c) Of what would this visible evidence be proof concerning this system of things?

7. (a) Is there some single event, by itself, that would be proof that "the end" is at hand? (b) How do we know when summer is near? So how can we know when the Kingdom has begun its rule?

Jesus told his disciples what would be visible proof
of his invisible presence in kingly power

they are already in the bud, by observing it you know for yourselves that now the summer is near. In this way you also, when you see these things occurring, know that the kingdom of God is near." (Luke 21:29-31) If we see one tree put out its leaves in midwinter because the weather is warm for a few days, we do not reason that summer has come, do we? But when we see *all* the trees budding and the days growing longer we know that summer has to be near. Likewise, when *all* the things that Jesus described take place, we can know for sure that Christ is on his heavenly throne and that his kingdom has, indeed, begun active rule. When that happens, liberation is near!

FULFILLMENT OF "THE SIGN"

[8] Exactly what did Jesus point to as marking his second presence and the "conclusion of the system of things"? He said: "Nation will rise against nation and kingdom against kingdom, and there will be food shortages and earthquakes in one place after another." (Matthew 24:7) Here Jesus tells us to look for a new kind of warfare —total war! The war that began in 1914 fits his description. Not only did armies fight on the battlefields; civilian populations too were organized to give full support to the war. As Jesus foretold, entire nations and kingdoms were fighting against one another. For the first time in history the whole world was at war. Hence it is called "World War I." Of it the book *World War I* said:

"In its scope, its violence, and above all, in its totality, it established a precedent. World War I

8. (a) As recorded at Matthew 24:7, what did Jesus say would mark his second presence? (b) Why did the war that began in 1914 fit his description? (c) So what year marked the beginning of the "last days" and the time when God's kingdom began its active rule?

ushered in the century of Total War, of—in the
first full sense of the term—global war.

"Never before 1914-1918 had a war absorbed
so much of the total resources of so many comba-
tants and covered so large a part of the earth.
Never had so many nations been involved. Never
had the slaughter been so comprehensive and
indiscriminate."*

The World Book Encyclopedia noted that the
number of soldiers killed and wounded was over
37,000,000, and added:

"The number of civilian deaths in areas of actual
war totaled about 5,000,000. Starvation, disease,
and exposure accounted for about 80 of every 100 of
these civilian deaths. Spanish influenza, which some
persons blamed on the war, caused tens of millions
of other deaths."†

This was just as Jesus foretold. Put together, these
facts mark 1914 as the beginning of the "last
days" and the year that God's heavenly kingdom
began its active rule.—See also Luke 21:10, 11.

⁹ Also, after 1914 a series of earthquakes rocked
the earth, causing great damage. In 1915, in
Italy, nearly 30,000 were killed. In 1920, in China,
180,000 died. In 1923, 143,000 died in Japan. And
major earthquakes have continued to take place
with unusual frequency since then. As Jesus foretold, they are another mark of the "last days."

¹⁰ However, Jesus said that the events that
marked the beginning of the "last days" in 1914
were only the "beginning of pangs of distress."
(Matthew 24:8) Greater trouble was to come.
True to his prophecy, it did. *The World Book*

* *World War I*, by H. W. Baldwin, 1962, pp. 1, 2.
† *The World Book Encyclopedia*, 1966, Vol. 20, p. 377.

9. What other event marking the "last days" has taken place
with unusual frequency since 1914?
10. What shows that the events that marked 1914 were only
the "beginning of pangs of distress"?

Encyclopedia says: "World War I and its aftermath led to the greatest economic depression in history during the early 1930's. The consequences of the war and the problems of adjustment to peace led to unrest in almost every nation." This paved the way for World War II. And of that war the same source notes:

"World War II killed more persons, cost more money, damaged more property, affected more people ... than any other war in history. ... It has been estimated that the number of war dead, civilian and military, totaled more than 22,000,000. The number of wounded has been estimated as more than 34,000,000."*

Truly, the "pangs of distress" Jesus foretold have become greater as the "last days" move toward their climax.

[11] During and after World War II widespread food shortages added to the distress. Shortly after the war *Look* magazine observed:

"A fourth of the world is starving today. Tomorrow will even be worse. Famine over most of the world now is more terrible than most of us can imagine. ... There are now more people hunting desperately for food than at any other time in history."†

More recently, the book entitled "Famine—1975!" said concerning today's food shortages:

"Hunger is rampant throughout country after country, continent after continent around the undeveloped belt of the tropics and subtropics. Today's crisis can move in only one direction —toward catastrophe. Today hungry nations; tomorrow starving nations.

---

* *The World Book Encyclopedia*, 1966, Vol. 20, pp. 379, 380, 410.

† *Look*, June 11, 1946.

---

11. (a) To what extent have food shortages added to the distress, as Jesus foretold? (b) What does the book entitled "Famine—1975!" say about the future?

"By 1975 civil disorder, anarchy, military dicta-
torships, runaway inflation, transportation break-
downs and chaotic unrest will be the order of
the day in many of the hungry nations."*

[12] Jesus also foretold the "increasing of lawlessness" as a mark of the "last days." (Matthew 24:
12) And God inspired the apostle Paul to add:
"In the last days . . . men will be lovers of themselves, . . . disobedient to parents, . . . without self-
control, fierce, without love of goodness, . . . lovers
of pleasures rather than lovers of God, . . . wicked
men and impostors will advance from bad to
worse." (2 Timothy 3:1-5, 13) These are the conditions that have developed at an explosive rate
since 1914! You have seen them with your own
eyes, have you not? Throughout the world lawlessness is running wild. Said one lawyer: "Almost
everywhere, including Soviet Russia, there appears to be an increase in crime, and particularly,
alas, in juvenile crime."† From nation after nation
come reports such as the following:

"A wave of crime and rioting is sweeping across
the United States . . . In many cities, women are
afraid to go out after dark. And they have good
reason. Rapes, assaults, sadistic outbursts of sense-
less violence are on the rise. Crimes often seem to
be committed out of sheer savagery . . . Respect for
law and order is declining."‡

[13] As another feature of the "last days," Jesus
spoke of great confusion and fear among the nations and their leaders. He foretold: "On the earth

* *Famine—1975!*, by W. & P. Paddock, 1967, pp. 52, 55, 61.
† *U.S. News & World Report*, Nov. 1, 1965, p. 80.
‡ *Ibid.*, Aug. 1, 1966, pp. 46, 47.

12. (a) What other conditions, foretold in the Bible, have
developed at an explosive rate since 1914? (b) So what kind
of reports come from nation after nation?
13. (a) At Luke 21:25, 26, what other feature of the "last days"
did Jesus foretell? (b) How is the fulfillment of this prophecy
evident in the news of our time?

anguish of nations, not knowing the way out . . .
men become faint out of fear and expectation of
the things coming upon the inhabited earth."
(Luke 21:25, 26) The fulfillment of this prophecy
is evident in the news of our time. *U.S. News
& World Report* said:

> "Is the world in greater tumult than before
> World War II? No doubt.
> "Shooting troubles, on the average, erupt *once
> a month*. Counting out real wars like Korea and
> Vietnam, the record still shows *over 300* revolutions,
> coups, uprisings, rebellions and insurrections world-
> wide since the end of World War II."*

Added to all these things is the fear of being
destroyed by the huge supply of nuclear weapons
some nations possess. One news editor commented: "The fact is that today the biggest single emo-
tion which dominates our lives is fear."† It is
just as Jesus foretold: mankind is fearful and the
nations are in anguish.

14 All the foretold marks of the "last days" are
here. They prove beyond a doubt that we have
been in the "last days" since 1914. Hence it was
in that year that God's heavenly kingdom came to
power!—Revelation 11:17, 18.

15 It is true that in past generations there were
periods marked by violence and much immoral
conduct. The decline of the Roman Empire is an
example. But never before in human history have
all the conditions specified by Jesus been observed
in the same generation. And never before have
they existed at the same time in every nation of
the earth. Today we live, not merely in the last

---

* *U.S. News & World Report,* Nov. 27, 1967, p. 62.
† *Ibid.,* Oct. 11, 1965, p. 144.

14. What does all the evidence show as to the year 1914?
15. Why is our generation unlike all others?

days of one political empire, but in the "last days" of the entire wicked system controlled by Satan.

1914 A MARKED YEAR

[16] Years in advance Bible scholars realized that 1914 was to be a year of great significance. Bible chronology specifically points to that year,* and careful students of God's Word knew that. They expected great changes to take place, and the facts confirm that 1914 was, indeed, a marked year.

[17] Others with knowledge of world affairs fully agree that 1914 was a marked year. The London *Evening Star* commented that World War I "tore the whole world's political setup apart. Nothing could ever be the same again. . . . some historian in the next century may well conclude that the day the world went mad was August 4, 1914."† Of the great change 1914 made, the historian H. R. Trevor-Roper said:

> "It is instructive to compare the first World War with the second . . . the first war marked a far greater change in history. It closed a long era of general peace and began a new age of violence in which the second war is simply an episode. Since 1914 the world has had a new character: a character of international anarchy. . . . Thus the first World War marks a turning point in modern history."‡

[18] World leaders have also commented on the significance of the year 1914. Former chancellor of West Germany Konrad Adenauer spoke of the

---

* For details concerning this, see the book *"Babylon the Great Has Fallen!" God's Kingdom Rules!*, pages 174-181; also *From Paradise Lost to Paradise Regained*, page 173.

† London *Evening Star*, quoted in New Orleans *Times-Picayune*, Aug. 5, 1960.

‡ The New York *Times Magazine*, Aug. 1, 1954, p. 9.

16. Did Bible scholars know in advance that there would be great changes in 1914?
17. What do historians say about the year 1914?
18. What have others said about the significance of 1914?

time "before 1914 when there was real peace, quiet and security on this earth—a time when we didn't know fear." Then he added: "Security and quiet have disappeared from the lives of men since 1914. And peace? Since 1914, the Germans have not known real peace nor has much of mankind."* Note, too, the comment in the book entitled "1914." The author says: "In the year 1914 the world, as it was known and accepted then, came to an end. Far more than any year before or since was this the punctuation-mark of the twentieth century . . . from then on nothing could ever be the same."†

19 Satan the Devil and his demons know they have only "a short period of time" left before their destruction. (Revelation 12:12) Even when Jesus was on earth, the demons knew that someday they would be destroyed. They showed a vicious disposition back then, and now that they know their time is short they are more vicious and desperate than ever. (Luke 8:27-33) They are out to stir up all the trouble that they can, in order to direct the attention of mankind away from the kingdom of God. That is why this wicked system of things has been behaving so crazily since 1914. It is behaving like a top, a child's toy, that wobbles crazily just before it tumbles to a complete stop.

20 Are we disheartened by this situation? Jesus said that his disciples would have reason to lift their heads up. Why? Because they realize the meaning of it all. They see in these events proof

* Cleveland *West Parker,* Jan. 20, 1966, p. 1.
† *1914,* by J. Cameron, 1959, pp. v, vi.

19. Why has this wicked system of things behaved so crazily since 1914?
20. (a) Why should we not be disheartened by the world situation? (b) What did Jesus foretell that his followers would be preaching at this time? Is it being done?

that deliverance is near! (Luke 21:28) And they do not keep this joyful news to themselves, but in all the earth they are preaching the thrilling news that the kingdom of God now rules. As Jesus foretold: "This good news of the kingdom will be preached in all the inhabited earth for a witness to all the nations; and then the end will come." (Matthew 24:14) This, too, is part of the "sign." In North and South America, Europe, Africa, Asia and the islands of the seas Jehovah's witnesses zealously keep proclaiming this urgent message. In both large cities and small villages you will find them, in all parts of the earth. Yes, this part of the "sign" is also being fulfilled.

[21] Beyond all doubt, the evidence points to 1914 as the year when the kingdom of God went into operation, and that event is causing things to happen here on earth. In that same year "the present wicked system of things" entered its "last days." (Galatians 1:4) Soon, now, the prayer for God's kingdom to "come" will be answered, when it displays its great power by destroying Satan's entire wicked system. Then God's kingdom alone will operate as the one government to rule the earth throughout eternity. (Daniel 2:44) Taking direct control of all earth's affairs, it will shower down on obedient mankind blessings of peace, happiness and life. The prayer for 'God's will to take place, as in heaven, also upon earth,' will have had glorious fulfillment, for God's kingdom will have come to rule forever. And think of it! *You* may enjoy eternal life under the loving rule of that kingdom. —Matthew 6:9, 10.

---

21. (a) Explain just what took place in 1914. (b) What will the answer to the prayer for God's kingdom to "come" mean?

CHAPTER 11

The Last Days of This Wicked System of Things

THE Bible speaks of the time in which we are living as the "last days" or the "time of the end." (2 Timothy 3:1; Daniel 11:40) The facts show that this is a limited period that has a definite beginning and a definite end. It began in 1914 when Jesus Christ was enthroned as king in the heavens. It will end when God destroys this present wicked system of things. What a relief it will be when the organizations and persons that cheat and oppress, and all who endanger the security of their fellowmen, are gone!

2 How soon will that be? God's own Son, Jesus Christ, gives the answer. After drawing attention to the many things that mark the period from 1914 onward as the "time of the end," Jesus said: "This generation will by no means pass away until all these things occur." (Matthew 24:34) Which generation did he mean?

3 Jesus had just referred to persons who would "see all these things." "These things" are the events that have taken place since 1914 and those

---

1. When did the "last days" begin, and with what event will they end?
2. What did Jesus say at Matthew 24:34 as to when the "time of the end" would run out?
3. (a) Which generation did Jesus say would not pass away before the end comes? (b) So how can we tell we are very near the end of this wicked system?

yet to occur down to the end of this wicked system. (Matthew 24:33) Persons born even as much as fifty years ago could not see "*all* these things." They came on the scene after the foretold events were already under way. But there are people still living who were alive in 1914 and saw what was happening then and who were old enough that they still remember those events. This generation is getting up in years now. A great number of them have already passed away in death. Yet Jesus very pointedly said: "This generation will *by no means* pass away until all these things occur." Some of them will still be alive to see the end of this wicked system. This means that only a short time is left before the end comes! (Psalm 90:10 [89:10, *Dy*]) So now is the time to take urgent action if you do not want to be swept away with this wicked system.

WHY A "TIME OF THE END"

⁴ Although the Kingdom came to power in 1914, Jehovah did not immediately destroy those who were not serving him. How glad we can be of that! For God's long-suffering has afforded us the

4. (a) Why can we be glad that God did not immediately destroy those who were not serving him when his kingdom came to power in 1914? (b) How does the Bible, at 2 Peter 3:9, help us to view this matter properly?

WITHIN ONE GENERATION

1914

END OF WICKED SYSTEM

Increase of lawlessness. Nation against nation. Earthquakes. Food shortages. Anguish of nations, not knowing the way out.

Critical times. Disobedience to parents. Not open to any agreement. Men without self-control.

"LAST DAYS"

opportunity to take a firm stand for his kingdom, and so escape destruction. The Bible helps us to view this matter in the proper light, saying: "Jehovah is not slow respecting his promise, as some people consider slowness, but he is patient with you because he does not desire any to be destroyed but desires all to attain to repentance."—2 Peter 3:9; see also Matthew 24:21, 22.

⁵ To this end, Jehovah God has allowed time for a separating work during these "last days." In his description of the "conclusion of the system of things," Jesus foretold this, saying: "When the Son of man [Jesus Christ] arrives in his glory, and all the angels with him, then he will sit down on his glorious throne. And all the nations will be gathered before him, and he will separate people one from another, just as a shepherd separates the sheep from the goats. And he will put the sheep on his right hand, but the goats on his left. Then the king will say to those on his right, 'Come, you who have my Father's blessing, inherit the kingdom prepared for you from the founding of the world.' . . . Then he will say, in turn, to those on his left, 'Be on your way from me, you who have been cursed, into the everlasting fire [of destruction] prepared for the Devil and his angels.' . . . And these will depart into everlasting cutting-off, but the righteous ones into everlasting life." (Matthew 25:31-46) When judgment is executed at the conclusion of these "last days," the ones destroyed will go into "everlasting cutting-off." There will be no return to life by a resurrection for them. (2 Thessalonians 1: 7-9) So, now, during these "last days," God has

5. (a) How did Jesus describe the separating work he would do at this time? (b) What happens to those against whom judgment is executed at the conclusion of these "last days"?

graciously given men everywhere opportunity to choose the side of his kingdom and live.

⁶ How does God do this? How is the separating work accomplished? Under angelic direction God's loyal servants throughout the earth proclaim the message of God's kingdom so that honest-hearted persons can hear and act upon it. This is the work that Jesus foretold as part of the "sign" indicating the nearness of the end, saying: "Also, in all the nations the good news has to be preached first." (Mark 13:10; see also Matthew 24:14 and Revelation 14:6, 7.) On the basis of their response to this message, and of their attitude toward those whom Jehovah uses as his messengers, the people are judged as to whether they will be preserved alive or not. (Matthew 25:40, 45) If you want life under the kingdom of God, it is vital to show it now by responding favorably to the Kingdom message and urging others to do the same. In the near future this preaching work will be finished. The door of opportunity will be closed. Then it will be too late!—Ezekiel 33:8, 9.

WHO WILL BE DESTROYED?

⁷ In frank terms the Scriptures reveal that, when this wicked system comes to its end, "those slain by Jehovah will certainly come to be . . . from one end of the earth clear to the other end of the earth." (Jeremiah 25:33) But you do not have to be among the slain. In his Word the Bible God clearly states what kind of persons, systems and organizations will be destroyed. Being forewarned, persons who love life, and who sincerely

6. (a) How is the separating work accomplished? (b) So, what must we do now if we want life under God's kingdom?
7. How does Jeremiah 25:33 describe the end of this wicked system, and how does the Bible help us to avoid being among those slain?

want to do what is right in the eyes of God, can get out of the danger zone.

⁸ So, then, who does God say will be destroyed? As we might expect, it is the wicked. "When the wicked ones sprout as the vegetation and all the practicers of what is hurtful blossom forth, it is that they may be annihilated forever." (Psalm 92:7 [91:8, *Dy*]) But let us not be misled by adopting the world's viewpoint as to what is righteous and what is wicked. God plainly tells us that much of what this world views as commonplace is wicked in his eyes. Fornication, adultery and homosexuality may be tolerated by modern-day society, but those who practice such things will not be spared alive by God at the end of this system of things. Likewise, those who are liars, thieves, drunkards and murderers will be barred from the realm of God's kingdom. (1 Corinthians 6:9, 10; Revelation 21:8) Some may have become involved in such practices because of bad associations. But now, knowing what God says, it is vital for these to change their ways if they want to avoid destruction. In God's new system there will be no place for persons who corrupt and cheat and who endanger the lives of their fellowmen.

⁹ Nor will there be any organizations that mislead the people. We have already learned from the Bible that not all religion is approved by God. So it should not surprise us that religion built on falsehood will become a thing of the past. A religious organization may have beautiful buildings and colorful rituals, but if it does not teach the

---

8. (a) Who does God say will be destroyed? (b) What kinds of persons does God classify as wicked? Can they change their ways?
9. (a) What will happen to religion built on falsehood, and why? (b) If we do not want to be numbered among those enemies of God, what must we do?

truth about God it really serves the purpose of the enemy of God, Satan the Devil. (1 Corinthians 10:20; 2 Corinthians 11:13-15) It may make some use of God's Word, but if it seeks to be a part of the world by having a say in worldly affairs, then, as the Bible declares, it becomes "an enemy of God." (James 4:4; John 15:19) Do we want to be numbered among God's enemies? If not, it is up to us to prove to God now that we are not in sympathy with them, that we find pleasure only in the truth and that we ourselves practice worship that is "clean and undefiled from the standpoint of our God and Father."—James 1:27.

[10] Also in line for destruction is the political system that has so cruelly oppressed mankind. As any study of history reveals, this system has a record of bloodshed and greedy grasping for power. Fittingly, God's Word compares the entire political arrangement on earth to a "wild beast," and it explains why the governments have manifested beastly qualities. It tells us that Satan the Devil, "the dragon," has given the worldly governments their power and that they operate under his control. (Revelation 13:2; Daniel 8:20, 21; Luke 4:5-8) God makes this information available to us so that we can decide intelligently as to whether we will have anything to do with the political affairs of the world or not. God also informs us what *he* will do. In Daniel 2:44 he speaks of the time when "the God of heaven will set up a kingdom that will never be brought to ruin." That took place in 1914 C.E. But, as to the action that God's kingdom will take in the near future, in the war of Armageddon or Har–Ma-

10. (a) Why will God destroy the entire political system on earth? (b) So, with what decision are we individually confronted?

gedon, he goes on to say: "It will crush and put an
end to all these kingdoms [existing at the time of
the end], and it itself will stand to times indefinite."—See also Revelation 16:14, 16; 19:17-21.

[11] After Satan's entire visible system has been
crushed, Jehovah will next turn his attention to
Satan the Devil, the god of this wicked system. He
will crush Satan, and he will do this soon. (2 Corinthians 4:4; Romans 16:20) At the time the
Devil was ousted from heaven following the establishment of the Kingdom in 1914, Satan knew
that he had only "a short period of time." (Revelation 12:12) Now that time is even shorter. Soon
the prophetic vision recorded at Revelation 20:1-3
will be fulfilled: "I saw an angel coming down out
of heaven with the key of the abyss and a great
chain in his hand. And he seized the dragon, the
original serpent, who is the Devil and Satan, . . .
And he hurled him into the abyss and shut it and
sealed it over him." So Satan, together with his
demons, will be taken out of the way. Their influence will be gone. This present wicked system
of things, in all its parts, will have come to its end.

[12] True Christians here on earth will have no
part in that destruction. It is God's war. He will
use angelic forces under Christ to carry out the
execution. He will also cause one part of Satan's
visible organization to turn on the other in violent
hatred. But Jehovah's servants on earth are not
to join in the violence. (2 Corinthians 10:3, 4)
Even when persecution is directed against them,

---

11. (a) After the visible part of this wicked system has been
crushed, to whom will God turn his attention? (b) How is this
described at Revelation 20:1-3?
12. (a) Will true Christians have any part in that destruction?
Whom will God use to execute judgment? (b) When persecution is directed against them, how should Jehovah's servants
respond?

they must not retaliate by seeking revenge against the rulers or trying to overthrow the government. They wait on God. "Do not avenge yourselves, beloved, but yield place to the wrath; for it is written: 'Vengeance is mine; I will repay, says Jehovah.' "—Romans 12:19.

WHAT WILL NEVER END

[13] The end of this system of things will not be the end for this planet earth. God's own Word guarantees: "The earth abideth for ever." "He has founded the earth upon its established places; it will not be made to totter to time indefinite, or forever." (Ecclesiastes 1:4, *AV;* Psalm 104:5 [103:5, *Dy*]) It is not the earth that is at fault, but the wicked system upon it.

[14] Furthermore, not all human life will come to an end. "Ungodly men" will be destroyed. (2 Peter 3:7) The people who made up the unbelieving world will be gone. But, after stating this, 1 John 2:17 adds: "He that does the will of God remains forever." It was to make this possible that Jesus Christ gave his life on behalf of mankind.—Hebrews 5:9.

[15] The marvelous prospect of eternal life under the righteous kingdom of God awaits the survivors of the end of this wicked system of things. Will you be one of them? You may well be. But, if so, you must "do your utmost" now, so that God's Word will deeply influence your entire life. (2 Peter 3:13, 14; Romans 12:1, 2) How thankful we can be that Jehovah, in his love and mercy, has made provision for survival!

---

13. Will the earth be destroyed when this system ends?
14. What kind of people will be gone, but who will remain?
15. To survive the end of this wicked system and live in God's new system, what must we do now?

CHAPTER 12

Righteous Rule Makes Earth a Paradise

HOW much mankind needs a righteous rule over all the earth! Everyone must agree that this planet today is no paradise. Poverty and hunger are the daily experience of millions of persons. Ugly cities rob earth of much of its natural beauty and poison the air and water around them. More and more cities are becoming 'jungles' of crime, where people are afraid to leave their homes at night. How different this is from God's original purpose for man! But how good it is to know that God has not abandoned his purpose! For he assures us: "My word that goes forth from my mouth . . . will not return to me without results." (Isaiah 55:11; see also Genesis 2:8, 15; 1:28.) He will yet make this earth a glorious paradise.

² Jehovah will soon bring to its end all the present wicked system. If you gain Jehovah's approval now, you may be privileged to survive into God's new system. What will this mean for you?

A RIGHTEOUS ADMINISTRATION

³ Mankind's greatest need, for nearly six thousand years, has been to be brought back into full harmony with Jehovah God, his Creator. (2 Co-

---

1. (a) What conditions show the need for a righteous rule over all the earth? (b) Will God yet make the earth a paradise?
2. How may we survive into God's new system?
3. What is God's means for restoring righteousness?

rinthians 5:20) To restore righteousness to this planet Jehovah himself has made provision for "an administration at the full limit of the appointed times." This administration or rule is by Christ's kingdom. As we have seen, the Kingdom has already come to power in the heavens and will soon take full charge of earth's affairs. What is its main purpose in doing this? "To gather all things together again in the Christ, the things in the heavens and the things on the earth." (Ephesians 1:9, 10) This administration is God's means for bringing all those living on earth into full harmony with his heavenly rule. This is what we pray for when we say: "Let your kingdom come. Let your will take place, as in heaven, also upon earth."—Matthew 6:10.

[4] What will this mean with regard to human relations? United in pure worship of their heavenly Father, people of all races and nationalities will live together as one family of brothers and sisters! (Acts 10:34, 35; 17:26) With God's kingdom by his "Prince of Peace" ruling over the entire globe, the earth will no longer be divided politically. There will be no proud nationalism to arouse hatred, conflict and bloodshed. (Isaiah 9:6, 7) Any death-dealing weapons of war that remain after Armageddon will soon be destroyed forever. (Ezekiel 39:9, 10; Psalm 46:8, 9 [45:9, 10, *Dy*]) So there will be no more newspaper lists of war casualties, no more war widows or war orphans, no more homes and cities bombed into ruins. What a blessing this will be for mankind!

[5] From his heavenly throne Jesus Christ will

4. (a) What changes will the Kingdom bring to human relations? (b) Why will there be no more war, and what will this mean to mankind?
5. Under Christ's rule, why will there be no injustice?

administer earth's affairs in a way that will bring lasting benefits. How wonderfully he has already demonstrated his qualifications, even laying down his own life on behalf of those who will be his subjects! Furthermore, the Bible record shows that nothing—temptations, pressures, reproach, even death itself—could turn Jesus aside from doing what is right. We can be sure, then, that under his rule there will be no oppression, injustice or corruption.—Isaiah 11:2-5.

⁶ Would you not appreciate, also, a ruler who always speaks the truth? Jesus is that kind of person. (John 1:14; 18:37) And who would not feel drawn to one who shows genuine warmth and sincere interest in others? When Jesus traveled about declaring the good news, the Bible tells us, he freely used the power that God had given him to heal the sick, both physically and in a spiritual way. (Matthew 9:35, 36) While it would have been grand to live during the time of Jesus' earthly ministry, it will be far grander to live on earth when he uses this power on behalf of all mankind.

⁷ Associated with Jesus in his heavenly kingdom will be 144,000 kings and priests taken from among mankind and made perfect by God. (Revelation 5:10) These, too, are persons who prove their love of righteousness down to the death.—Revelation 14:1, 4, 5; 2:10.

⁸ But will this heavenly government have any visible representatives? Yes, indeed! Why, even now the heavenly administration appoints faithful men as its representatives in the Christian con-

---

6. What kind of person is Jesus, so that we should be grateful to have him as Ruler?
7. What kind of persons are those who will rule with Jesus in his heavenly kingdom?
8. (a) Will there be visible representatives of Christ's heavenly kingdom? (b) Who will select them?

gregation, doing so by means of God's holy spirit. (Isaiah 32:1, 2; Acts 20:28) So we can be confident that Christ will see to it that the right men on earth are assigned to represent the Kingdom government, for then he will be taking a direct hand in earth's affairs. Because these men represent the King in a special way, the Bible calls them "princes." These will all have proved their loyalty to God and their love for their fellowmen. The same spirit of God that motivates their heavenly King will also guide them.—Psalm 45:16 [44:17, *Dy*].

⁹ Neither race, nor color, nor place of birth will have any bearing on the way these princely representatives apply God's righteous laws. (Deuteronomy 10:17; Romans 2:11) Following the example of their King, the "princes" will serve humbly and helpfully, bringing refreshment to their fellowmen. Yet they will be firm in upholding God's righteousness.—Matthew 11:29; 20:25-28.

¹⁰ The earth having been cleansed of all evildoers, crime will never be allowed to take root again. (Psalm 37:9-11 [36:9-11, *Dy*]) Never again will there be a need for policemen, jails, handcuffs, burglar alarms, safes, locks and keys. Under the Kingdom's righteous rule, you will know that anyone knocking at your door is a friend. There will be complete freedom from fear of any harm. Nevermore will anyone be afraid to stroll through a park at night to view the starry handiwork of the Creator. Even as is true of God's congregation today in a spiritual way, so then in a literal way,

9. Will the color of one's skin or his place of birth influence how he is treated then?
10. In contrast with the insecurity and fear so common today, what will be the conditions under Christ's righteous rule?

"they will actually dwell in security, with no one
to make them tremble."—Ezekiel 34:28.

FREEDOM FROM SIN BRINGS
HEALTH AND LIFE

[11] The initial program of the Kingdom will cover
a period of one thousand years. During that time
Jesus Christ and the members of his heavenly
government will serve not only as kings but also
as priests of God on behalf of all their human subjects. (Revelation 20:6) Why? Because all persons
on earth will need to be "set free from enslave-
ment to corruption" in order to have "the glorious
freedom of the children of God." (Romans 8:21)
Even after the wicked have been destroyed, the
earthly survivors will still be imperfect due to sin
inherited from Adam. The wrong desires of their
imperfect flesh will still be warring against the
right desires of mind and heart. (Romans 7:21-23)
So, to be accepted fully into God's family of sons,
they first need the services of the heavenly priests
of God. What will these do?

[12] They will have a power that has been lacking
in all human governments till now: the power to
cleanse persons of sin and imperfection. This
power rests in God's heavenly priesthood by means
of Jesus' ransom sacrifice. God's Son and his associate priests will then apply the benefits of Jesus'
sacrifice directly to all obedient ones. (John 1:29;
1 John 2:2) This provision is pictured in the Bible
by the symbolic "river of water of life" that flows
from the "throne of God and of the Lamb" and
"the leaves of the trees . . . for the curing of the

---

11. Besides serving as kings, in what other capacity will the
members of Christ's heavenly government serve? Why?
12. (a) What unique power will the members of Christ's
heavenly kingdom have? (b) To what blessed state will people
attain?

nations." (Revelation 22:1, 2) By making continual progress in righteousness and with the help of the heavenly priesthood, they will progressively grow young and strong, until they reach perfection of health in mind and body. They will be set completely free from the bondage to sin and death inherited from Adam.—John 11:26.

[13] Yes, in this way, God will "wipe out every tear from their eyes, and death will be no more, neither will mourning nor outcry nor pain be any more. The former things have passed away." (Revelation 21:4) How marvelous it will be to enjoy perfect health! Even as God's Son cured lepers and healed the lame and blind when on earth, so his righteous rule will bring an end to all disease and suffering. (Mark 1:40-42; John 5: 5-9; Matthew 9:35) Gone then will be the need for hospitals and health insurance! With sickness and death removed, a worldwide cause for tears will be gone. (1 Corinthians 15:25, 26) How wonderful it will be to enjoy full freedom from sin, and to be able to measure up perfectly to God's righteous standards in speech, thought and conduct!

WELCOMING PERSONS BACK FROM THE DEAD

[14] There is also the happy prospect that your loved ones who have died will be able to enjoy the blessings of the righteous rule of God's Son over the earth. Jesus revealed the hope for the countless millions who have died, saying: "Do not marvel at this, for the hour is coming in which all those in the memorial tombs will hear his voice

13. (a) How does Revelation 21:4 describe the blessings the Kingdom will bring? (b) What did Jesus do when he was on earth that shows he can bring about these blessings?
14. What prospect for the dead did Jesus reveal at John 5:28, 29?

Even the dead were raised to life by Jesus

and come out." (John 5:28, 29) What a time of thrilling joy it will be when first the news is flashed around the earth: "The dead are being raised up!"

[15] We can have full confidence that this will be a reality. Keep in mind that, while on earth, Jesus not only cured the sick and crippled; he also brought dead persons back to life. (Matthew 11: 2-6) This demonstrated God's wonderful power of resurrecting the dead, a power he has granted to Jesus Christ. Perhaps you recall the occasion when Jesus came to the house of a man whose twelve-year-old daughter had died. Addressing himself to the dead girl, Jesus said: "Maiden, I say to you, Get up!" What was the result? The Bible tells us: "Immediately the maiden rose and began walking." How did her parents and the

15. Why can we have confidence that Jesus will raise the dead?

other observers react to this miracle? "At once they were beside themselves with great ecstasy." They could hardly contain their happiness.—Mark 5:35, 38-42; see also John 11:38-44; Luke 7:11-16.

[16] When paradise is restored to earth, Jesus will again use his power to raise the dead. For the Bible assures us that "there is going to be a resurrection of both the righteous and the unrighteous." (Acts 24:15) What joy there will be earth wide when group after group of dead persons come back to life! Imagine what happy reunions of loved relatives there will be! Instead of obituary columns, there may well be announcements of newly resurrected ones to bring joy to their loved ones.

[17] Many millions of persons have died, but that poses no problem for God. He can remember them all. Why, the Bible tells us that God "is counting the number of the stars; all of them he calls by their names." (Psalm 147:4 [146:4, Dy]) Consider what that means. There are said to be hundreds of millions of galaxies, each galaxy containing hundreds of millions of individual stars, and yet God knows each star by name. The number of all the humans that have ever lived is small by comparison. So it will not be difficult for God to remember all who have died and who come under Christ's ransom provision. (Matthew 19:26) They will be restored to life right here on earth. What a thrilling privilege to be on hand to welcome them back from the dead!

[18] When they come back will they be the same persons? Will we know them? Yes! Even man can

16. Who will be raised from the dead, and how will this affect the living?
17. Why is it no problem for God to remember all those who are to be resurrected?
18. In the resurrection, will you be able to recognize those you knew before? Why?

indefinitely preserve pictures and voices on magnetic tape for later use on television. God can do even more than that. At resurrection time he can provide each one with a suitable body, just as he did in creating the first man, and then reimplant in the brain the exact memories of all that the person learned and experienced during his former life. Thus in the resurrection that person will come forth with the same personality that he had at death, just as the resurrected Jesus retained his own personality. (Hebrews 13:8) You will recognize those you knew before. What a wonderful prospect!—Job 14:13-15.

[19] The apostle John was given a vision of these thrilling events that will take place during Christ's reign, and it is found in the book of Revelation. His vision shows that death and Hades (mankind's common grave) will 'give up those dead in them.' None will be left there. Then death due to inherited sin will be gone forever. (Revelation 20:13, 14; Isaiah 25:8) Gone will be funeral parlors and tombstones! No graveyards will remain to mar the beauty of the paradise earth.

[20] Those resurrected to life on earth will come forth to the opportunity of gaining eternal life in paradise. It will be a time of education for them. "Scrolls" containing instruction from God will be opened, and they will need to follow these in making their minds over in harmony with God's will. They will be "judged individually according to their deeds"; that is, the deeds they do after being resurrected and after learning the contents

19. What does the book of Revelation show as to the dead? So what will be gone?
20. (a) What opportunity will be open to the resurrected ones, and what will they need to do? (b) On what basis will they be judged? (c) How will changes take place in the ways of persons who may previously have been dangerous?

of the "scrolls." (Revelation 20:11-13) By responding to the education provided, even those who were once as dangerous as wild animals will change their ways, just as many have already done upon coming into association with the Christian congregation.—Isaiah 11:9; 26:9; 35:8, 9.

EARTH RETURNS TO PARADISE CONDITIONS

[21] Progress in righteousness will bring material blessings too. There will be a literal fulfillment of the prophetic words of Isaiah 25:6: "And Jehovah of armies will certainly make for all the peoples, in this mountain, a banquet of well-oiled dishes." None will ever again know the gnawing pain and weakness of starvation. But how will God provide this banquet?

[22] When the Israelites were God's chosen people, his blessing brought them great prosperity. Their lands produced fine crops of grain. Their orchards grew excellent fruits. Jehovah opened up to them his "good storehouse, the heavens, to give the rain on [their] land in its season." (Deuteronomy 28: 12; see also verse 8.) Similar blessings will abound in fullest measure under the rule of Christ's kingdom. (Psalm 67:6, 7 [66:7, 8, *Dy*]) The earthly subjects of the Kingdom will fulfill the command that Adam and Eve never carried out. They will "subdue" the earth, making the entire globe a paradise. It was concerning such a prospect, and with the hope of resurrection in view, that Jesus said to the sympathetic evildoer who was executed with him: "Truly I tell you today, You will be with me in Paradise."—Luke 23:39-43.

21. What blessing of the Kingdom rule is described at Isaiah 25:6?
22. (a) As shown in the Bible, how will this material plenty be provided? (b) To what condition will the entire globe be transformed?

²³ Then the whole earth will radiate happiness. It will be as if its meadows and mountains, its trees and flowers, its rivers and seas, are all rejoicing at Jehovah's righteous rule. (Psalm 96: 11-13 [95:11-13, *Dy*]; 98:7-9 [97:7-9, *Dy*]) The fresh air will no longer suffer contamination. Every river and stream will sparkle with fresh, pure water. There will be no more ruining of the land.

²⁴ All earth—its forests, its fields, its mountains —will be one beautiful park, alive with colorful varieties of animals and birds. These, too, will be subject to the wise control of Jehovah's Son. And in that "inhabited earth to come" he will bring them all into harmless subjection to mankind. —Hebrews 2:5-8; Psalm 8:4-8 [8:5-9, *Dy*].

FINAL TEST DETERMINES WORTHINESS
FOR ETERNAL LIFE

²⁵ God's kingdom by Christ will rule for all eternity. However, by the close of the first thousand years it will have accomplished a particular purpose toward the earth. It will have removed every trace of unrighteousness. All humankind on earth will stand as perfect creatures before the throne of the Supreme Judge, Jehovah God. In every respect they will be equal to the first perfect humans in Eden. (1 Corinthians 15:24) Will they be worthy to have God grant them the right to everlasting life? It will be proper that the Kingdom subjects be tested as to their devotion to God's righteous rule. Jehovah will give them the oppor-

---

23. How do the Psalms describe the happy condition that will prevail on earth?
24. What will Christ's rule do for mankind with regard to the animal creation?
25. (a) By the close of the first thousand years, what will the Kingdom have accomplished? (b) What test will then take place, and why?

tunity to show their loyalty. How? By releasing Satan and his demons from their condition of restraint in the "abyss." (Revelation 20:7) By this test each one in God's earthly family may individually have the privilege of giving a personal answer to the challenge made to their heavenly Father by Satan.

[26] Those who stay loyal to God will be judged worthy of everlasting life. Jehovah will give this right to them, writing their names in his "book of life." Any who rebelliously turn against God will be destroyed in the "second death." Then, Satan the Devil, along with his demons, will be destroyed forever. (Revelation 20:7-10, 15) Never, no, never, will the earth, or any other part of God's vast universe, be disturbed again by sin and rebellion. Made into a paradise where righteousness prevails, the earth will serve for all time to come as a jewel of praise to Jehovah's name.

[27] Does God's purpose for a righteous rule over a paradise earth deepen your respect for his righteousness? Does it increase your appreciation of his wisdom? Does it move you to express your love for him? If so, then you should do all you can now to serve him wholeheartedly. Share in telling others of Jehovah's name and purpose. (Psalm 89:14-16 [88:15-17, Dy]; 1 John 4:19) Live now according to God's righteous principles, and so prepare for life eternal in the paradise earth under the Kingdom's righteous rule.

26. What will be the outcome for (a) those who stay loyal to God? (b) those who turn against God? (c) Satan and his demons?
27. If we really want life in the paradise earth, what should we do now?

CHAPTER 13

The True Church and Its Foundation

IF WE want to live eternally in God's new system
we must acknowledge the true church and its
foundation. With reference to them, Jesus said:
"Upon this rock I will build my Church." (Matthew 16:18, *Dy*) What is this church and what is
the rock upon which it is built? The Bible provides
us with the right answers.

² While many persons speak of the buildings in
which people meet for worship as "churches," did
you know that the Bible never does? In the Bible
the word "church" always refers to people, actually to an assembly or congregation of persons.
(Philemon 2) The Greek word *ek·kle·si'a*, translated "church" or "congregation," literally means
"that which is called out." It refers to a group
of persons called out from among others for a particular purpose; but it is used as the equivalent
of the Hebrew word *qahal'*, meaning "congregation" or "assembly."

³ The true church or congregation is likened to
a human body, because it has many members but
only one head, just as a human body has. The

1. Why is it important to know the identity of the true church
and its foundation?
2. (a) Does the Bible ever use the word "church" to refer to a
building? (b) What is the meaning of the Greek word?
3. Why is the true church likened to (a) a human body? (b) an
engaged virgin girl?

inspired Scriptures, at Ephesians 1:22, 23 (*Dy*), tell us that God made Christ "head over all the church, which is his body." This church is also compared to a virgin girl engaged to Christ, because as a group the members of the true church are to be closely united to Christ, as a wife is to her husband. Writing to certain members of the church, the apostle Paul said: "I personally promised you in marriage to one husband that I might present you as a chaste virgin to the Christ." (2 Corinthians 11:2; see also Revelation 21:2, 9, 10.) So it is a clean congregation, free from worldly corruption and devoted to its Head, Jesus Christ.

[4] Could anyone of us decide to "join" this church simply by getting his name placed on some membership roll here on earth? No; as Hebrews 12:23 (*Dy*) explains, this is the "church of the firstborn who are *written in the heavens*." God is the one who selects the members. He sets them in the congregation as *he* pleases. (1 Corinthians 12:18) These are the ones who will be with Christ in heaven. And Jesus revealed that, far from including all who profess to be Christians, they are limited in number to 144,000.—Revelation 14:1-3; Luke 12:32.

[5] They are, indeed, a group of persons called out from spiritual darkness for a special purpose. While here on earth they boldly "declare abroad the excellencies" of the Most High God, who called them out of darkness into his wonderful light. (1 Peter 2:9) And, after their resurrection, they will have the grand privilege of ruling with Christ in his heavenly kingdom.—Luke 22:28-30.

---

4. (a) Can anyone "join" the true church by getting his name on some earthly membership roll? Why? (b) How many make up the true church that will be with Christ in heaven?
5. For what special purpose are members of the true church called?

⁶ The first members of this true church were all Jews (as were Jesus and his apostles) or circumcised Jewish converts. At Pentecost of 33 C.E. —just ten days after Jesus had ascended to heaven and opened the way for others to follow him in due time—Jehovah indicated his selection of these members through the pouring out of holy spirit. Their receiving of the spirit on that occasion bore witness to them that they were now God's spiritual sons and heirs of the kingdom with Christ. (Acts 2:1-4, 16-21, 33; Romans 8:16, 17) But the membership of the true church did not remain all Jewish. Three and a half years after Jesus' death the way was opened for Gentiles or non-Jews to be included. (Acts 10:30-33, 44; Romans 9:23, 24) So, in course of time, the true church came to have international membership.

THE FOUNDATION OF THE TRUE CHURCH

⁷ Who is the foundation of the true church? Jesus Christ made clear that he himself is that foundation. He applied to himself the prophecy of Psalm 118:22 [117:22, *Dy*], saying: "The stone that the builders rejected is the one that has become the chief cornerstone." (Matthew 21:42-44) The apostle Paul adds his testimony that Jesus is the "chief corner stone," writing to Christians at Ephesus: "You are fellow citizens with the saints and the domestics of God, built upon the foundation of the apostles and prophets, Jesus Christ himself being the chief corner stone." (Ephesians 2:19, 20, *Dy*) The apostle was very definite about it, saying again: "For other foundation no man

6. (a) Who were the first members of the true church, and how was witness borne to them that they were God's spiritual sons? (b) When was membership opened up for non-Jews?
7. How did Jesus and the apostle Paul identify the foundation cornerstone of the true church?

can lay, but that which is laid: which is Christ Jesus."—1 Corinthians 3:11, *Dy*.

[8] There could be no finer and surer foundation for the true church than Christ Jesus, could there? It is his own perfect human life given as a ransom that makes possible this divine arrangement. Yet, how can we harmonize this testimony by Jesus and the apostle Paul with what Jesus stated to Peter at Matthew 16:18? We may be sure that there is no contradiction.

"UPON THIS ROCK I WILL BUILD MY CHURCH"

[9] Peter had just acknowledged Jesus to be the Christ (or, the Messiah), the Son of the living God. Jesus then said: "I say to thee: That thou art Peter, and upon this rock I will build my Church." (*Dy*) Some understand these words to mean that Jesus' church is built on Peter as the foundation. This is the official position of the Roman Catholic Church. But it is of interest to note that Archbishop Kenrick, in the book *An Inside View of the Vatican Council* (1870), shows that of at least eighty-six early church "fathers," only seventeen understood Jesus' reference to the "rock" as applying to Peter. Were you aware of this?

[10] Consider, for example, the view of Augustine (354-430 C.E.), usually referred to as "Saint Augustine." Though at one time he viewed Peter as the "rock," in later life Augustine restated his position, saying in his *Retractationes:* "I have since frequently explained the words of our Lord: 'Thou art Peter and upon this rock I will build my

8. (a) Why could there be no finer foundation for the true church than Christ Jesus? (b) What question now comes up?
9. (a) How do some persons understand Jesus' words at Matthew 16:18? (b) Did the majority of the early church "fathers" understand Jesus' reference to the "rock" as applying to Peter?
10. How did Augustine understand Jesus' reference to the "rock"?

Church,' to the effect that they should be understood as referring to him whom Peter confessed when he said: 'Thou art the Christ, the Son of the living God,' . . . For what was said to [Peter] was not 'Thou art the rock,' but 'Thou art Peter.' But the rock was Christ."

[11] But of far more importance—how did Peter himself understand Jesus' words? Concerning the Lord Jesus, Peter said: "Unto whom coming, as to a living stone, rejected indeed by men but chosen and made honourable by God: Be you also as living stones built up, a spiritual house, a holy priesthood, to offer up spiritual sacrifices, acceptable to God by Jesus Christ. Wherefore it is said in the scripture: Behold, I lay in Sion a *chief corner stone,* elect, precious. And he that shall believe in him shall not be confounded. To you therefore that believe, he is honour: but to them that believe not, the stone which the builders rejected, the same is made the head of the corner: and a stone of stumbling and a *rock* of scandal, to them who stumble at the word." (1 Peter 2:4-8, *Dy*) These words of Peter show that he, like the apostle Paul, understood Jesus to be the "chief corner stone," the "rock" on which the church is built. Peter is just one of the 144,000 "living stones" making up the true church.

[12] Peter enjoyed fine privileges as an apostle of Jesus Christ, it is true. But nowhere does he indicate that he thought he was the chief of the apostles. Nor do we read anywhere that the other apostles and disciples recognized Peter as a "pope" and gave him honor as such. On one occasion the

11. Whom did Peter himself understand to be the "rock"?
12. (a) How do we know whether Peter was viewed as an "infallible" head of the early church? (b) Who always remains the head of the true church?

apostle Paul found it necessary to reprove Peter (Cephas) publicly for having taken a course not in keeping with true Christian faith. The fact that Peter was wrong on this matter involving faith and morals and also that Paul felt free to correct him publicly shows that Peter was not looked to as an "infallible" head of the apostles or of the early church. (Galatians 2:11-14) In the true church there is only one Head, Jesus Christ, who, since his resurrection, is "alive forever," and so needs no successors.—Hebrews 7:23-25.

A UNITED CHURCH

[13] Jesus, the Head, does not split up the body of his congregation into a clergy class and a laity class of the "common people." He says to his followers: "Do not you be called Rabbi, for one is your teacher, whereas all you are brothers. Moreover, do not call anyone your father on earth, for one is your Father, the heavenly One. Neither be called 'leaders,' for your Leader is one, the Christ." (Matthew 23:8-10) So Jesus shows that there is no division among those who make up the true church. However, he did arrange for men to take the lead in the Christian congregation, to serve the spiritual needs of their brothers and organize the work of preaching the good news. Jesus said such ones were not to "lord it over" their brothers but were to be like slaves or servants to them. (Matthew 20:25-28) Is that true of the clergymen you know?

[14] To fit the Bible's description of the true church, those who make it up must be united in

their worship. In this regard the apostle Paul wrote: "I exhort you, brothers, through the name of our Lord Jesus Christ that you should all speak in agreement, and that there should not be divisions among you, but that you may be fitly united in the same mind and in the same line of thought." (1 Corinthians 1:10) So we cannot Scripturally expect to find them scattered among all the conflicting religions of Christendom. They must be gathered together in just one organization. As Ephesians 4:4, 5 says of them: "One body there is, . . . one Lord, one faith." It is vital for us to know what that "one faith" is.

APPRECIATION OF THE TRUE CHURCH AND ITS FOUNDATION

[15] The members of the true church under Christ their head are said to become "Abraham's seed, heirs with reference to a promise." (Galatians 3: 29) This promise is that all others of obedient mankind will bless themselves through Christ and his congregation. (Genesis 22:18) The Bible foretold that, at the time of the establishment of Christ's kingdom, there would be only a remnant of these children of the "Jerusalem above," God's heavenly organization, left on earth. (Galatians 4: 26; Revelation 12:10, 17) Jesus described these members of his church on earth as a "faithful and discreet slave." And he said that such ones who were found faithfully serving at the time of his coming to his judgment work would be appointed "over all his belongings," that is, over all the earthly interests of Christ's kingdom. They would take the lead in the preaching of the good news of the

---

15. (a) How do Christ and his congregation benefit all other obedient humans? (b) What responsibility did Jesus say he would give to his true church at the time of his coming in Kingdom power?

established Kingdom to all the nations in the "time of the end."—Matthew 24:14, 45-47; 25:19-23.

[16] All those today who hope to gain eternal life in God's new system need to recognize this arrangement. For Jesus said that, in this "time of the end," he separates to a position of favor those doing good to the remaining ones on earth of his "brothers," his joint heirs who make up the Christian congregation. (Matthew 25:31-40) These are the remaining ones of the "living stones" that are built up into a spiritual house or temple, "a place for God to inhabit by spirit." (1 Peter 2:5; Ephesians 2:20-22) Those 'doing good' to the members of this temple class are described in the book of Revelation as a "great crowd" of persons who come under God's protection. Note, too, that they gladly serve God "day and night in his temple," that is, in association with the remnant of the spiritual temple class, the Christian congregation. —Revelation 7:9, 10, 15.

[17] These sheeplike persons say, in effect, to the heirs of the promise made with Abraham: "We will go with you people, for we have heard that God is with you people." (Zechariah 8:23) Even as those of the true church or congregation faithfully walk in Christ's footsteps and proclaim the Kingdom message, so likewise these sheeplike ones 'go with them,' serving God right along with them. Are you doing that? If so, you have the prospect of receiving eternal life on earth, along with all the other blessings that will flow from Christ and his glorified congregation in the heavens.

16. What blessings come to those who show proper recognition of this arrangement?
17. What do sheeplike ones say, in effect, to the remaining ones of the true church?

CHAPTER 14

How to Identify the True Religion

L OGICALLY there must be just one true religion. This is in harmony with the fact that the true God is a God, "not of disorder, but of peace." (1 Corinthians 14:33) Furthermore, Jesus Christ spoke of those who practice such religion as worshiping God "with spirit and truth," and truth is never at disagreement with itself. (John 4:23, 24) But who are these true worshipers today? How can you identify them and know that their worship is indeed the one approved by God?

² This cannot be decided simply on the basis of what people and organizations *claim* to be. In his Sermon on the Mount, Jesus pointed out that many would call him "Lord, Lord," claiming to have done notable things in his name. Yet he would say to them: "I never knew you! Get away from me, you workers of lawlessness." Not only words but also appearances can be deceptive. Jesus said that false prophets would come in sheep's covering, while inside they would be like devouring wolves. However, he gave us a rule by which we can distinguish between the true servants of God

1. Why is it both logical and Scriptural to say that there is just one true religion?
2. (a) Are all who profess to be Christians practicing the true religion? (b) What rule did Jesus give by which we can distinguish between God's true servants and the false ones?

and the false ones, saying: "By their fruits you will recognize them." He showed that what really determines whether we are true worshipers of God is not merely our claims or even our apparently commendable works, but our actually doing the will of the heavenly Father.—Matthew 7:15-23.

[3] A faithful follower of Jesus, the apostle Paul, also showed the need for caution. He warned that some men would appear to be ministers of righteousness and yet would be false Christians. Outwardly they may not seem bad. But when measured in the light of God's Word, the Bible, they are shown to be ministers of God's enemy, Satan, for their works are actually in opposition to God's will. (2 Corinthians 11:13-15) Our following the lead of such false Christians could only result in our losing out on life eternal.

APPLYING THE RULE

[4] What, then, are some of the identifying marks of true worshipers of God? What are the fine fruits that they would produce? The Bible tells us that "God is love." In harmony with this, Jesus showed that the most outstanding mark of those who follow his example in worshiping God is that *they would have love among themselves*. He said: "By this all will know that you are my disciples, if you have love among yourselves." (1 John 4:8; John 13:35) For such love to be truly an identifying mark, it could not be merely a matter of pretending to be nice to one another, could it? It must be love that deeply affects every aspect of one's daily living. It should influence how one treats the other members of one's household. It

3. What warning set out by the apostle Paul shows the need for caution?
4. What is the most outstanding mark of the true worshipers of God?

ought to affect one's attitude toward people of
other races and nations. True worshipers of God
show love, not only in word, but also in action.
They seek what is truly in the best interests of
others.—1 John 3:18.

⁵ Do the religious organizations with which you
have been acquainted have this mark of identifi-
cation? Do they instill in their members a love
that is so strong that it remains true even in
difficult times? What do they do, for example,
when tension between worldly nations leads to
war? The facts show that by far the majority of
them have been willing for their members to go
out on the battlefield and slaughter their fellow
believers of another nationality at the command
of worldly men. Do you think such a course is
according to God's Word and really reflects the
spirit of God?—1 John 3:10-12; Matthew 5:44.

⁶ Yet, as you know, not everyone has followed
this course. Some have been able to say with the
apostle Paul: "For though we walk in the flesh,
we do not wage warfare according to what we are
in the flesh. For the weapons of our warfare are
not fleshly." (2 Corinthians 10:3, 4) They have
not been guilty of living a lie by saying, "I love
God," while hating their brother of another nationality. (1 John 4:20, 21) Those who truly imitate Jesus, not only refrain from doing harm to
others, but also manifest love in other ways. How?
By their unity with fellow Christians in all lands,
by the way they deal with their neighbors and by
their loving efforts to help others to learn about
God.—Galatians 6:10.

5. How do religious organizations and their members today measure up with regard to this main mark of true religion?
6. (a) Are there persons who have shown true Christian love
even in times of worldly conflict? (b) How is their love more
than a mere refraining from doing harm to others?

⁷ Another mark of true religion and of those who practice it is *respect for God's Word*. God's Son when on earth set the pattern in this by showing the highest respect for the inspired Scriptures. He quoted them as the final authority on matters. He continually referred his hearers to God's Word, encouraging them to read and apply it. (Matthew 19:4-6; Luke 24:44, 45) He showed his deep respect for the Bible by living in accord with its teachings every day. The fulfillment of God's Word meant more to him than even his own life. (Matthew 26:53-56) Never did he downgrade the Bible; rather, he condemned those who failed to teach in harmony with it and who tried to weaken its force with their own teachings.—Mark 7:9-13.

⁸ What can we say in this regard about the many church organizations of Christendom today? When you hear or read statements by clergymen who refer to parts of the Bible as "myths," or who favor the theory of evolution over the Bible teaching of creation, would you say that they are encouraging respect for God's Word? Or when you read statements in which such church leaders argue that sex relations outside of marriage are not necessarily wrong, or that even homosexuality can be quite proper, would you say that they are encouraging people to use the Bible as their guide? They certainly are not following the example of God's Son and his apostles.—Matthew 15:18, 19; Galatians 5:19-21; Romans 1:24-27.

⁹ Do the fruits manifest in the lives of the mem-

---

7. What viewpoint toward the Bible does true religion encourage, and how did God's Son set the pattern in this?
8. What kind of statements by clergymen of Christendom indicate that they are not following the example of God's Son and his apostles in this matter?
9. Why is the worship of even many who have the Bible not pleasing to God?

bers of these churches show that they truly respect the Word of God? From your own experience, would you say that most people who go to a church building on Sunday apply Bible principles in their home life and in their dealings with others on Monday and during the rest of the week? God's Word shows that there are persons who may have the Bible and even study it but whose works prove that they disown the God they claim to know. (Titus 1:16; John 5:39, 40) The form of worship that they practice is not pleasing to God, because they do not allow his Word to exercise genuine power in their lives.—2 Timothy 3:5.

[10] At first one might reason that it is simply one minister who is wrong or certain church members who do not do right. But what if the minister who downgrades the Bible continues to hold his position? And what if the church members who do wrong continue to be in good standing? Then it is time to face the fact that the bad fruits identify the religious organization itself. If that is true, you will, without exception, find that the teachings of the organization do not all line up with the Bible. If you have read the previous chapters of this book and considered the Bible texts found there, you may realize that this is true of the religion with which you have been associated. If so, then you have a serious problem. It is the problem of making a decision either to accept the truthfulness of the Bible or to reject it in favor of teachings that the Bible does not support. (Acts 17:11) What you do, of course, must be your own decision. However, you should

---

10. (a) How can we know if the bad fruits identify not merely individuals, but the religious organization itself? (b) What serious decision must a person make if he has found that the teachings of his church do not all line up with the Bible?

weigh matters carefully, since the decision you make will affect your standing with God and your prospects of eternal life in his new system.

[11] A further requirement of true religion is that it must *sanctify God's name*. Why so? Because when Jesus Christ taught his followers how to pray, he showed them that this should be their first concern. "You must pray, then, this way," he said: "Our Father in the heavens, let your name be sanctified." (Matthew 6:9) This means holding the name sacred, treating it as something holy. Jesus himself certainly did this. He did not fail to use his Father's name, nor did he treat it as unimportant. To the contrary, in prayer to his Father, Jesus said: "I have made your name known to them and will make it known." (John 17:26) He knew that it is God's purpose for his name to be glorified in all the earth, and he set the example in proclaiming and honoring that name. (John 12:28; Isaiah 12:4, 5) Also, the Scriptures show that the main purpose for the existence of the congregation that God has called out of the world is to be "a people for his name." (Acts 15:14) If you are to gain salvation, you, too, must know and honor the name of God. —Romans 10:13, 14.

[12] Now, stop and ask yourself: What religious group is most prominently known for publishing the name of God, as Jesus did? The churches in general avoid the use of the name Jehovah; and, though some of them say that they favor the form "Yahweh," they seldom use that either. Some

---

11. (a) How does true religion treat God's name, as indicated by Jesus Christ? (b) So what must we do if we are to gain salvation?
12. (a) Are the churches in general measuring up to this requirement of true worship? (b) Are there any who bear witness to the name of God?

have even gone to the extent of removing God's name from their versions of the Bible. For example, the *Revised Standard Version,* which is now distributed with the backing of both Protestants and Catholics, omits the name Jehovah completely, although it appears in the original Hebrew text nearly seven thousand times. Are these organizations measuring up to this requirement of true religion? Really, what group does bear witness to the name of God, as Jesus did? (Revelation 1:5; Isaiah 43:10-12) If you were to talk to your neighbors and refer repeatedly to Jehovah, using his sacred name, with what organization do you think they would associate you? That is not a difficult question to answer. There is only one people that notably follow Jesus' example in this regard.

[13] True worshipers also proclaim *the kingdom of God as man's true hope.* They could not do otherwise and be pleasing to Jehovah God, because he has clearly stated that the Kingdom is his provision for governing the earth. (Daniel 2:44; 7:13, 14) Jesus set the example by going from one end of the land to the other "preaching and declaring the good news of the kingdom of God." (Luke 8:1) He and his apostles did this by going from village to village and "from house to house." (Acts 20:20) Jesus also foretold that in these "last days" "this good news of the kingdom" would be preached in all the earth for a witness.—Matthew 24:14.

[14] Today we often hear religious leaders speaking on behalf of political organizations such as the United Nations and praying for them. But who are

---

13. (a) What must true worshipers advocate as man's only hope? (b) How do they do this?

14. (a) Instead of God's kingdom, in favor of what do we often hear religious leaders speak and pray? (b) Who are the people that come to your door preaching the Kingdom as mankind's true hope?

doing the preaching of the good news about God's kingdom as Jesus foretold? If someone comes to your door or to your neighbor's door and you hear him talking about God's kingdom as mankind's true hope, with what organization do you associate that person? This is a principal activity of those who actually do the will of the heavenly Father in imitation of his Son Jesus.—1 Peter 2:21.

[15] Yet another requirement of true religion is that it keep *separate from the world and its affairs*. The Bible, at James 1:27, shows that, if our worship is to be clean and undefiled from the standpoint of God, we must keep ourselves "without spot from the world." This is an important matter, for, "whoever . . . wants to be a friend of the world is constituting himself an enemy of God." (James 4:4) You can appreciate why this is so serious when you remember that the Bible points out that the ruler of the world is God's chief adversary, Satan the Devil.—John 12:31.

[16] Do the facts show that the churches in your community take this to heart? Are the clergy, as well as the members of the congregations, really "no part of the world," as Jesus said that his true followers would be? (John 15:19) Or are they deeply involved in the world's affairs, in its nationalism, its politics and its class struggles? You do not need someone else to answer these questions for you. The activities of the churches are widely publicized, and you know what is going on in them. If there are people in your community who, because of their religion, refrain from such activities, you no doubt know who they are too.

15. Name another vital requirement of true religion, as explained at James 1:27.
16. From what you have observed, are the churches in your community, and their members, really "no part of the world"?

¹⁷ Now, after reviewing these identifying marks of the true religion that God has provided for us in his Word, what do we conclude? The question at issue is not whether a certain religious group appears to meet one or two of these requirements, nor whether *some* of its doctrines conform to the Bible. Far more than that, the true religion must measure up in all these respects and its teachings must all be in full harmony with God's Word. Only in this way can such religion truly be pleasing to Jehovah God. There are not many religions meeting these requirements. The Bible shows that there is only "one faith."—Ephesians 4:5.

¹⁸ Who, then, are the ones who form the body of true worshipers today? On the basis of the evidence, which is known or available to persons in all parts of the earth, we do not hesitate to say that they are the Christian witnesses of Jehovah. For you to share that conviction you need to get well acquainted with them. The best way is to attend their meetings at the Kingdom Hall of Jehovah's Witnesses. In this way you can observe for yourself how the organization functions and the way in which those associated with it apply God's Word in their own lives. Since God assures us that practicing true religion brings great contentment now and opens up the way for eternal life in his new system of things, it surely will be worth your while to make such an investigation. (Deuteronomy 30:19, 20) You have our warm invitation to do so. Why not investigate now?

---

17. (a) To be the true religion, to how many of these requirements must a religion conform? (b) As shown in the Bible, how many true religions are there?
18. (a) In the light of the evidence, whom does this book point to as the true worshipers today? Is that what you believe? (b) What is the best way to get well acquainted with Jehovah's witnesses?

CHAPTER 15

"Get Out from Among Them"

JEHOVAH GOD expects all who love and serve him to keep free from false worship. Of God's Son, the Bible says: "You loved righteousness, and you hated lawlessness." Because of this his Father has specially blessed him, exalting him as the appointed king of God's kingdom. (Hebrews 1:9) If you love truth and righteousness, then you will also hate and avoid what is false and displeasing to God. In this way you can find protection both now and during the coming execution of God's judgment upon those who disregard his will.

² Long ago God foretold that he would have a people who would be his "special property," and that observers would certainly see "the distinction between a righteous one and a wicked one, between one serving God and one who has not served him." (Malachi 3:17, 18) If you see this distinction, then you should act accordingly. Failure to do so would endanger your prospect of gaining life eternal. What course should you take? God's Word says very definitely: "Do not become unevenly yoked with unbelievers. For what sharing do righteousness and lawlessness have? Or what fellowship

1. If we love truth and righteousness, what must we also hate and avoid?
2. If we see the distinction between those serving God and those not serving him, what course should we take, and why?

131

does light have with darkness? . . . Or what portion does a faithful person have with an unbeliever?'' Because there can be no proper fellowship between those practicing righteousness and those practicing lawlessness, God commands: ''Therefore get out from among them, and separate yourselves.''—2 Corinthians 6:14-17.

GETTING OUT OF ''BABYLON THE GREAT''

[3] To those who were once his chosen people and who were in exile in ancient Babylon, Jehovah God spoke similar words: ''I, Jehovah, am your God, the One teaching you to benefit yourself, the One causing you to tread in the way in which you should walk. O if only you would actually pay attention to my commandments! Then your peace would become just like a river, and your righteousness like the waves of the sea. . . . One's name would not be cut off or be annihilated from before me. Go forth, you people, out of Babylon!'' (Isaiah 48:17-20) What Jehovah did there was for the benefit of those loving him, not to deprive them of anything good. By the conquest of Babylon in 539 B.C.E. he made it possible for them to leave Babylon as a free people.

[4] Ancient Babylon has ceased to exist. Yet God speaks of another Babylon called ''Babylon the Great.'' And again he gives the command: ''Get out of her, my people, if you do not want to share with her in her sins, and if you do not want to receive part of her plagues.'' (Revelation 18:4) In the previous chapter of Revelation, Babylon the Great is described in symbol as an immoral woman

3. What similar words did God speak to his exiled people in ancient Babylon, and was this depriving them of anything good?
4. (a) Though ancient Babylon no longer exists, what does God say about another Babylon? (b) In Revelation chapter 17, how is this greater Babylon pictured?

who sits over or controls "peoples and crowds and nations and tongues," and who has "a kingdom over the kings of the earth" and 'commits fornication' with these kings.—Revelation 17:1, 2, 15, 18.

⁵ This means that Babylon the Great is an empire. What kind of empire? Since "the kings of the earth," the political element, are said to 'commit fornication' with her, Babylon the Great itself is not a political empire. The book of Revelation shows that when Babylon the Great is destroyed the "merchants" of the earth stand at a distance and mourn; so it is not a commercial empire either. (Revelation 18:15) Could it, then, be a religious empire? Well, religion has certainly had great influence over the political kingdoms, and its control does extend over peoples of all the earth. But why should this religious empire be pictured by a prostitute woman guilty of fornication? Because it mixes religion and politics. As regards Christendom, the Bible shows that those who claim to serve God but are unfaithful and enter into relations with the political powers are viewed by God as spiritual prostitutes or adulteresses.—Ezekiel 16:1, 2, 28-30; James 4:4.

⁶ It was shortly after the global flood of Noah's day that false religion got its start in Babylon, where Nimrod exalted himself "in opposition to Jehovah." However, Jehovah confused the people's language and "scattered them from there over all the surface of the earth." As they went, they took with them their Babylonish doctrines and practices. (Genesis 10:8-10; 11:4-9) In harmony with

5. (a) Is Babylon the Great a political empire? (b) Why could Babylon the Great not be a commercial empire? (c) In the Bible, why would a religious empire be pictured by a prostitute woman?
6. Where did false religion get its start after the Flood, and how did its doctrines and practices become widespread?

this, the book *The Religion of Babylonia and Assyria* (by Professor Morris Jastrow, page 701) tells of "the profound impression made upon the ancient world by the remarkable manifestations of religious thought in Babylonia and by the religious activity that prevailed in that region."

[7] Thus, although many persons are unaware of it, there are many doctrines and practices found in religions throughout the earth today that have a common origin in Babylon's false religion. What are some of these?

[8] Among the teachings prominent in ancient Babylon were: worship of a triad or trinity of gods, the belief that the human soul could not die, and the teaching that persons suffered after death in an underground world or "land of no return." The use of images also played a large part in Babylonian worship. As has been shown in earlier chapters of this book, none of these things are taught in God's Word, the Bible. However, do we see similar teachings and practices in the religious organizations around us today?

[9] Along with the doctrines of the "Trinity," the immortality of the human soul and a hellfire of torment, any other teaching or practice that goes contrary to God's inspired Word marks a religion as false and labels it as part of Babylon the Great. A religion may *claim* to advocate worship of the true God of the Bible and it may use the name of his Son, Jesus Christ, but of what value is this if it is contaminated with Babylonish doctrines and

7. Where did many doctrines and practices found in religions today have their origin?
8. (a) Name some of the religious teachings prominent in ancient Babylon. (b) Are they taught in God's Word?
9. (a) What labels a religion as part of Babylon the Great? (b) Since God has foretold that he will bring sudden destruction upon Babylon the Great, what is it urgent to do?

practices? (Galatians 5:7-9; Matthew 7:22, 23) God has foretold that suddenly, "in one day," plagues of "death and mourning and famine" will come upon Babylon the Great. So it is urgent and for our good that we completely separate ourselves now from every part of that false religious empire. —Revelation 18:8.

¹⁰ What does it mean to "get out from among them"? Is it enough for a person merely to recognize in his mind the falseness of Babylonish teachings, while still continuing to associate with a religious organization that holds to those teachings? Really, would this not be a course of hypocrisy? Would it not give visible support to something that God condemns? How could such a person truly consider himself obedient to God's command to "get out from among them, and separate yourselves, . . . and quit touching the unclean thing"? (2 Corinthians 6:17) If we do not want to be like those people who gathered at the temple of Baal in Jehu's time only to suffer destruction at God's command, then we need to make a clean break from any and all organizations of Babylon the Great. We need to quit sharing in their activities. (2 Kings 10:20-27)* We need to serve notice on them that we are withdrawing from their organizations. By doing this we will not be "limping upon two different opinions," trying to 'partake of "the table of Jehovah" and the table of demons,' and thereby "inciting Jehovah to jealousy."—1 Kings 18:21;† 1 Corinthians 10:21, 22.

¹¹ But is not the getting together of religions in

---

* 4 Kings 10:20-27, *Dy*.   † 3 Kings 18:21, *Dy*.

10. (a) Is a person 'getting out from among them' if he continues to associate in any way with a religion that teaches false doctrines? (b) What notice should one serve on the religious organization with which he was formerly associated?
11. What is the Bible view of interfaith movements?

an interfaith or ecumenical movement a good thing? Well, how does Jehovah God view it? The Bible record shows that he allowed no interfaith with the Canaanites for the nation of Israel. (Deuteronomy 7:3, 4) And how did God's Son view interfaith? He did not engage in interfaith activities with the various sects of Judaism while on earth. To the contrary, he roundly condemned the false religion of his day, and stated positively: "No one comes to the Father except through me." —John 14:6; see also Matthew 23:13, 38.

FIRM STAND FOR TRUTH BRINGS BLESSINGS

[12] Making a clean break from false worship may bring problems. Jesus showed that one's relatives may oppose such a course. Yet, even though those opposing may be as near and dear as a member of one's own family, Jesus said that this should make no difference in our decision. (Matthew 10:32-37) It is a question, not of loving such ones less than formerly, but of how strong our love is for Jehovah and his Word of truth.

[13] Actually, it is by taking a firm stand for the truth that one can really act for the lasting good of relatives who may at first oppose one's right course. Yielding to pressure may only encourage these in their opposition to the truth. On the other hand, your faithful conduct in holding to the truth of God's Word and living in harmony with it will bring you blessings and happiness; it will make a better person of you. Thus, in course of time, those close to you may come to recognize the wisdom of your course and be helped to see the truth

---

12. (a) When one makes a clean break from false worship, what may happen with regard to one's relatives? (b) What love does this put to the test?
13. (a) What effect may your enduring in the truth have on persons close to you? (b) What assurance does God give?

as well. This is the hope the Bible encourages us to embrace and work for. (1 Corinthians 7:12-16; 1 Peter 3:1, 2) True, it will call for patience, faith that God's way is best, and, above all, love. But God himself lovingly assures you that he will support and strengthen you if you put him first in your life.—Romans 8:38, 39.

¹⁴ Again, some may feel that they are now well along in years, and that it is too late to change their course. However, Jehovah God, who is himself called "the Ancient of Days," invites old persons, also, to join in praising him. (Daniel 7:9; Psalm 148:12, 13) His Word shows that old age will not excuse one if one fails to separate from what God condemns, but that "gray-headedness is a crown of beauty when it is found in the way of righteousness." (Proverbs 16:31; see also Ezekiel 9:4-6.) It is never too late in life to take a stand in harmony with what one knows to be the truth, thus setting one's steps firmly on the way to eternal life.—Proverbs 10:22.

¹⁵ If we now take positive action to get out from among those who practice false religion, we may enjoy a blessed, happy relationship with our God, Jehovah. (2 Corinthians 6:17, 18) For the matter does not end with getting out from among those who teach and practice things contrary to God's Word. God also gives the command that we should not 'forsake the gathering of ourselves together,' as Hebrews 10:24, 25 tells us. With whom, then, are we to assemble? With those who worship God in spirit and in truth. Of such ones God says:

---

14. (a) Does God expect old persons to separate from false religion and take up true worship? (b) What prospect will this open up for such persons?
15. (a) What blessing can we enjoy if we get out from among those who practice false religion? (b) So, with whom are we to assemble?

"I shall reside among them and walk among them, and I shall be their God, and they will be my people."—2 Corinthians 6:16.

16 Those who make up the Christian organization of Jehovah's witnesses are persons who have separated themselves from the many religions of both pagandom and Christendom. They have thus fled from Babylon the Great. By attending meetings at one of their Kingdom Halls, you can see for yourself the difference this has made. It is not just the meeting place and the fact that money collections are not taken, but primarily the meetings themselves and the attitude of the persons attending that mark Jehovah's witnesses as distinct from other religions. These meetings are real Bible studies, with emphasis on how Bible principles apply in our daily lives and also on how to teach God's Word to others. There you will see persons who are sincerely 'seeking first the kingdom and God's righteousness,' and who earnestly endeavor to produce the fruits of God's spirit. —Matthew 6:33; Galatians 5:22, 23.

17 Attending once or twice may satisfy your curiosity, but for you to make genuine progress in God's service you need to be like the early Christians. They really valued the truth, so they "continued devoting themselves to the teaching of the apostles . . . And day after day they were in constant attendance at the temple with one accord." (Acts 2:42, 46) Only by regularly sharing in these congregation meetings can you develop the faith, appreciation and conviction that you need to gain God's approval.

---

16. By attending the meetings of Jehovah's witnesses, what will you observe regarding (a) money collections? (b) the meetings themselves? (c) the attitude of the persons attending?
17. Why is it important to share in these meetings regularly?

¹⁸ Although separating from modern Babylon the Great may cost you something in the way of previous associations, you will gain far more by your regular attendance at the meetings of Jehovah's people. Like Jesus' early disciples, who also left much in order to follow him, you will see fulfilled the promise to "get a hundredfold now in this period of time" in the way of brothers and sisters and homes where you will be gladly received. You will find that you have become part of a large family of Christian brothers, whose love and friendship are genuine and sincere. You will gain all this along with the hope of everlasting life "in the coming system of things."—Mark 10:28-30; Psalm 27:10 [26:10, *Dy*].

¹⁹ Jehovah God has a visible organization that he is using today to train and equip us for life in his righteous new system. After the present wicked system is gone, God's way will prevail everywhere. His will be the only government left. (Daniel 2:44) His approved people will be the only ones remaining on earth with whom to associate. Only God's standards of right and wrong will be allowed. There will be only one religion. So the wise thing to do is to bring ourselves into line with God's way of doing things now, taking full advantage of the training that God provides through His written word the Holy Bible. In this way we prove that we really mean it when we say that we want eternal life in God's righteous new system.—Psalm 86:10, 11 [85:10, 11, *Dy*]; Proverbs 4:10-13.

18. What promise of Jesus will be fulfilled toward you by your separating from Babylon the Great and regularly associating with Jehovah's people?
19. (a) How is God using his visible organization for our blessing? (b) So what is it wise for us to do now?

CHAPTER 16

Popular Customs That Displease God

W E HAVE everything worth while to gain and nothing of true value to lose by seeking to please God in all things. To him the psalmist says: "You will cause me to know the path of life. Rejoicing to satisfaction is with your face; there is pleasantness at your right hand forever." (Psalm 16:11 [15:11, *Dy*]) However, Satan the Devil tries to turn persons away from true worship and direct them into ways that displease Jehovah God. One of the means he uses to accomplish this is the practice of popular customs that go contrary to Bible teachings.

² Not all popular customs are wrong. But they are displeasing to God if they are rooted in false religion or if they are in some other way in conflict with Bible principles. (Matthew 15:6) Interestingly, most of the popular customs that have survived till today are of a religious nature. Since we have already seen that worldly religion has turned aside from the Bible's standard of pure worship, it should not surprise us to find that many of their customs are based on pagan religious practices.

1. By seeking to please God, do we gain or lose?
2. What determines whether a popular custom is wrong?

[3] In warning the Israelites against the religious customs of the surrounding nations, Jehovah told his people that they should "not learn the way of the nations at all." (Jeremiah 10:2) This was a loving warning, because those pagan customs were based on falsehood, misrepresenting God and his purpose. Often those customs had a bad effect on the morals of those practicing them. For a like reason the Bible counsels us today: "Quit being fashioned after this system of things, but be transformed by making your mind over, that you may prove to yourselves the good and acceptable and perfect will of God." (Romans 12:2) A sincere desire to please Jehovah God will help us to do so.

THE USE OF THE CROSS

[4] Many churchgoers wear a cross, or have a crucifix in the home, and crosses are found in many church buildings. But did you know that the cross actually has a pagan origin? The facts show that, rather than being the exclusive symbol of Christianity, the cross was in use centuries before the birth of Christ. This is admitted by *The Catholic Encyclopedia* (1908 edition, Vol. IV, page 517):

"The sign of the cross, represented in its simplest form by a crossing of two lines at right angles, greatly antedates, in both the East and the West, the introduction of Christianity. It goes back to a very remote period of human civilization."

[5] Showing the pagan religious origin of the cross, the book *The Ancient Church* by clergyman W. D. Killen says (1859 edition, page 316):

"From the most remote antiquity the cross was venerated in Egypt and Syria; it was held in equal

3. (a) What warning did Jehovah give his people against pagan religious customs? (b) How can we be helped to apply the counsel found at Romans 12:2?
4. What does *The Catholic Encyclopedia* admit about the cross?
5. What does the book *The Ancient Church* say about the pagan origin of the cross?

honour by the Buddhists of the East; . . . about the commencement of our era, the pagans were wont to make the sign of a cross upon the forehead in the celebration of some of their sacred mysteries."

[6] And, further showing its connection with Babylonish religion, W. E. Vine, in *An Expository Dictionary of New Testament Words* (Vol. 1, page 256), says that the cross "had its origin in ancient Chaldea [Babylon], and was used as the symbol of the god Tammuz (being in the shape of the mystic Tau [or T], the initial of his name)."

[7] But was not Jesus put to death on a two-beamed cross? The Bible indicates that he was not. At Acts 5:30 and 10:39, in both Catholic and Protestant Bible translations, we are told that Jesus died on a "tree." The word "tree" here translates the Greek word *xylon* (or *xulon*). Concerning this word and the word *stauros,* translated "cross" in some versions, *The Companion Bible* says on page 186 in the "Appendixes":

"Homer [ancient Greek poet] uses the word *stauros* of an ordinary pole or stake, or a single piece of timber. And this is the meaning and usage of the word throughout the Greek classics. It never means *two* pieces of timber placed across one another at any angle, but always of one piece alone. Hence the use of the word *xulon* [or *xylon,* meaning a timber] in connection with the manner of our Lord's death, . . . The evidence is thus complete, that the Lord was put to death upon an upright stake, and not on two pieces of timber placed at any angle."

[8] Showing how and when such use of the cross began among professed Christians, W. E. Vine, in his book, says:

---

6. Where did the cross have its origin, and of what god was it a symbol?
7. (a) According to the Bible book of Acts, was Jesus put to death on a two-beamed cross? (b) How do ancient Greek writers use the word that is translated "cross" in some Bible versions?
8. When did the use of the cross begin among professed Christians? And why did they adopt a pagan sign?

"By the middle of the 3rd century A.D. the churches had either departed from, or had [made a distorted imitation of], certain doctrines of the Christian faith. In order to increase the prestige of the apostate ecclesiastical system pagans were received into the churches apart from regeneration by faith, and were permitted largely to retain their pagan signs and symbols. Hence the Tau or T, . . . with the cross-piece lowered, was adopted to stand for the cross of Christ."—Vol. 1, page 256.

[9] It is not normal to cherish and adore the instrument used to murder someone we love. Who would think of kissing the revolver that had been used to murder a loved one, or of wearing it around one's neck? This being so, and the cross being proved to be a pagan religious symbol, persons who have worn such an object or had crucifixes in their homes, thinking that this honored God and his Son Jesus Christ, are faced with an important decision. Will they continue to use them? Will they even keep them? Love of the truth and the desire to please God in *all* things will help in making the right decision.—Deuteronomy 7:26.

RELIGIOUS IMAGES AND PICTURES

[10] Ever since the time of ancient Egypt and Babylon, the use of religious images, shrines and pictures in the home has been popular. These have been cherished by persons who believed that they would bring safety and blessing to their homes. But is Jehovah pleased with this practice? Does he approve of those who look to material objects of devotion instead of putting full trust in him, the true and living God?

---

9. (a) Is it normal to cherish an instrument used to murder a loved one? (b) If one has been using a cross, what decision must he make? What will help in making the right decision?
10. (a) How far back does the use of religious images, shrines and pictures date? (b) In this connection, what questions deserve our consideration?

¹¹ Showing his displeasure with religious images as aids to devotion, God gave his law to the Israelites forbidding their use. Moreover, he warned them against desiring the gold and silver on images they found among pagan peoples. (Exodus 20:4, 5; Deuteronomy 7:25) Did God's attitude change with the introduction of Christianity? No, for the Bible shows that Christians likewise avoided the use of images. (Acts 17:29) Following the apostle John's counsel to "guard yourselves from idols," they walked "by faith, not by sight." They put their complete trust in the invisible God. —1 John 5:21; 2 Corinthians 5:7.

¹² Secular history agrees with this. As M'Clintock and Strong's *Cyclopædia* (Vol. IV, page 503) tells us: "Images were unknown in the worship of the primitive Christians." Since the early Christians kept their homes free from religious images, where did images of Christ get started? The book *The History of the Christian Religion and Church, During the Three First Centuries* (by Dr. Augustus Neander) (Second edition, 1848, page 183) tells us: "Heathens, who, like Alexander Severus [Roman emperor of the third century C.E.], saw something Divine in Christ, and sects, which mixed heathenism and Christianity together, were the first who made use of images of Christ." Since no images of Christ were used by the early Christians, it is evident also that they had no images of Mary, Jesus' mother.

¹³ Does this mean that it is wrong to have any

11. (a) Did God allow the ancient Israelites to use religious images as aids to devotion? (b) Why did the early Christians also avoid the use of images?
12. How did images of Christ get started? So, did early Christians have images of Jesus' mother?
13. (a) What determines whether a statue or picture displeases God? (b) What is the origin of the halo or "nimbus"?

art object, such as pictures or statues, in the home? No, for there is a difference between mere objects of art and objects of religious devotion. What is it that determines whether a statue or picture is displeasing to God? This: is it reverenced or worshiped, perhaps candles or food being placed before it, as in some countries? Does it misrepresent the Bible? Or does it portray pagan symbols? You may have noticed that some pictures of Jesus Christ have a circle of light around his head. This is called a halo or nimbus. If you look up "nimbus" in an encyclopedia, you will learn that it was used by ancient Egyptians, Greeks and Romans in their pagan religious art. The halo can be traced back to Babylonian sun-worship, and it appears with representations of gods of Babylon.

[14] Do we have guidance from the past as to what we should do if we find such religious images and pictures in our midst? Well, what did faithful Jacob do when he found false gods among the members of his household? He got rid of them. (Genesis 35:2-4) And what did young King Josiah do as a result of starting to search for the true God? He cleaned the graven images out of Judah, breaking them to pieces. (2 Chronicles 34:3, 4)* What fine examples of zeal in giving glory to Jehovah God!—Psalm 115:1-8, 18 [113:1-8, 18, second set of numbers, *Dy*].

HONORING HUMANS AND INSTITUTIONS

[15] In many places it is the custom to set aside days to honor "saints," or famous persons, dead

---

* 2 Paralipomenon 34:3, 4, *Dy*.

14. What did faithful servants of God in the past do when they found such false religious items in their midst?
15. (a) Are holidays that give worshipful honors to creatures pleasing to God? (b) Holidays in memory of the "spirits of the dead" are based on what false doctrine? So, what is the truth about All Souls' Day?

or alive. Is this pleasing to God? The Bible warns against giving worshipful honors to creatures, so holidays that tend in that direction are not in harmony with God's will. (Acts 10:25, 26; 14:11-15; Romans 1:25; Revelation 19:10) Further, holidays in memory of the "spirits of the dead" are actually based on the false doctrine of the immortality of the human soul. So it should not surprise us to read, in the *Encyclopædia Britannica* (1946 edition, Vol. 1, page 666), that "certain popular beliefs connected with All Souls' Day are of pagan origin." Persons who love the way of the truth are careful to avoid such celebrations.

[16] Other holidays or celebrations honor and exalt nations or worldly institutions. The wrong custom here is giving credit to such organizations for benefits that really should be credited to God, or crediting such institutions with the power to save and protect in a way that actually only God can do. (Jeremiah 17:5-7) So, participants in these celebrations play false to God. True Christians will be guided by the principle that they are to be "no part of the world." (John 15:19) Rather than imitate the world, they will "quit being fashioned after this system of things."—Romans 12:2.

[17] Some customs that may seem quite innocent lead in the same direction as the practices mentioned above. Thus, while the celebration of birthdays may seem of little consequence, they exalt the creature, making him the center of attention rather than the Creator. We should note, too, that

16. (a) What is wrong with holidays or celebrations that honor nations or worldly institutions? (b) How do the Scriptures show what course Christians should take?

17. (a) At a birthday celebration, who is exalted as the center of attention? (b) Who are the only persons whose birthday celebrations are reported in the Bible? (c) How did the early Christians view birthday celebrations?

the only two birthday celebrations mentioned in the Bible are those of Egypt's Pharaoh and Herod Antipas, rulers who followed false religion. (Genesis 40:20-22; Matthew 14:6-10) And what of the early Christians? Historian Neander says: "The notion of a *birthday festival* was far from the ideas of the Christians of this period in general." (Page 190) They shunned birthday celebrations as of pagan origin. Those who earnestly seek to please God wisely avoid customs that exalt any creature or that have their origin with false religion.—John 5:44.

EASTER AND CHRISTMAS

[18] Easter is Christendom's chief religious holiday, said to be held in memory of Christ's being raised from the dead. But did Christ give a command to celebrate his resurrection? No, he did not. History books tell us that Easter was not celebrated by early Christians and that it is based on ancient pagan practices. *The Encyclopædia Britannica* says:

> "There is no indication of the observance of the Easter festival in the New Testament. . . . The sanctity of special times was an idea absent from the minds of the first Christians."*

Dr. Alexander Hislop says of Easter customs:

> "The popular observances that still attend the period of its celebration amply confirm the testimony of history as to its Babylonian character. The hot cross buns of Good Friday, and the dyed eggs of Pasch or Easter Sunday, figured in the Chaldean [Babylonian] rites just as they do now."†

The word "Easter" that appears once in the King James Bible at Acts 12:4 is a wrong translation

---

* *The Encyclopædia Britannica*, 1910, Vol. VIII, p. 828.
† *The Two Babylons*, pp. 107, 108.

18. (a) Did the early Christians celebrate Easter? (b) What is the origin of Easter's popular customs? (c) Does the Easter celebration find any support at all in the Bible?

for the word "passover."* "Easter" appears nowhere in the Catholic Douay Bible. Christendom's chief holiday, Easter, therefore finds no support at all in the Bible. It is of pagan origin, and therefore displeasing to God.

[19] What about Christmas? By checking reference works in a public library, you will find that it was unknown among the earliest Christians. Jesus instructed his followers to observe a memorial of his death, not of his birth. (1 Corinthians 11:24-26) Says *The Catholic Encyclopedia:* "Christmas was not among the earliest festivals of the church. . . . The first evidence of the feast is from Egypt."†

[20] What, then, of the date December 25, celebrated by many as the birthday of Christ? It could not have been the date of Jesus' birth. The Bible shows that at the time shepherds were still in the fields at night. As the *Encyclopædia Britannica* (1907, Vol. V, p. 611) acknowledges, they would not have been there in the cold, rainy season of winter. (Luke 2:8-12) As for the origin of the date, *The World Book Encyclopedia* says:

"In A.D. 354, Bishop Liberius of Rome ordered the people to celebrate on December 25. He probably chose this date because the people of Rome already observed it as the Feast of Saturn, celebrating the birthday of the sun."‡

[21] Since the date of Christmas is of pagan origin,

---

* See modern Bible translations of Acts 12:4 or *The Westminster Dictionary of the Bible*, p. 145.
† *The Catholic Encyclopedia*, 1908, Vol. III, p. 724.
‡ *The World Book Encyclopedia*, 1966, Vol. 3, p. 416.

19. (a) Was Christmas celebrated by the earliest Christians? (b) What memorial did Jesus instruct his followers to keep?
20. (a) How do the facts show that Jesus could not have been born in the cold of winter? (b) When was the date December 25 chosen, and why that date?
21. What do the facts of history show as to the origin of most of the Christmas customs?

it should not seem strange that the customs of Christmas are also of pagan origin. Thus the *Encyclopædia of Religion and Ethics* tells us:

"Most of the Christmas customs now prevailing ... are not genuine Christian customs, but heathen customs which have been absorbed or tolerated by the Church. ... The Saturnalia in Rome provided the model for most of the *merry* customs of the Christmas time."*

Also, *The Encyclopedia Americana* points out that among the customs borrowed from the pagan Roman feast of Saturnalia was "the giving of gifts."†

²² There is no escaping it: Christmas is of pagan origin. Knowing this, we should pay attention to the apostle Paul's warning against mixing the true and the false. He says that even "a little leaven ferments the whole lump." (Galatians 5:9) He reproved some of the early Christians for observing days that had been kept under the law of Moses but that God had canceled for Christians. (Galatians 4:10, 11) How much more important it is for true Christians today to shun a celebration that was never authorized by God, that stems from pagan Babylon, and that falsely bears the name of Christ!

FINER THAN PAGAN CELEBRATIONS

²³ True Christians have something finer than pagan celebrations. They have the "fruitage of the spirit," which is "love, joy, peace, long-suffering,

---

* *Encyclopædia of Religion and Ethics,* by James Hastings, Vol. III, pp. 608, 609.
† *The Encyclopedia Americana,* 1956, Vol. VI, p. 622.

22. (a) How should Galatians 5:9 influence our attitude toward Christmas? (b) For what sound reasons do true Christians shun the celebration?
23. What do true Christians have that is finer than the once-a-year "Christmas spirit"?

kindness, goodness, faith, mildness, self-control."
(Galatians 5:22, 23) This fruitage produces a
generosity that is much more beautiful and genuine than the "Christmas spirit" that blooms just
once a year. God's spirit produces kindness and
unselfishness that can plainly be seen every day
of the year. This prompts Christians to give, not
with the hope of repayment or because they are
pressured into it, but out of genuine Christian
love.—Luke 6:35, 36; Acts 20:35.

[24] Real Christians can give gifts and have good
times together throughout the year. (Luke 6:38)
Parents do not have to wait for birthdays or for
Christmas, but they can bring gifts to their children at various times during the year. This makes
for many happy occasions instead of one or two.
Further, the children know that it is their parents
who are giving them the gifts, doing so out of love
for them. This helps to cement the bond of love
between parents and children. Moreover, children
are not encouraged to be unthankful to man or
God, because of thinking that they are entitled
to receive gifts on certain days.—Colossians 3:14.

[25] Learning the truth about the pagan origins
of popular customs can have a marvelous liberat-
ing effect. No longer do we feel obligated to follow
practices that have proved to be a burden, finan-
cially and otherwise, to people of the world. And,
most important, our knowing the truth frees us
to pursue the course that is pleasing to Jehovah,
so that we may find everlasting life in his righteous new system.—John 8:32; Romans 6:21, 22.

---

24. (a) When do real Christians give gifts and have good times
together? (b) How is this better than what the world does?
25. Learning the truth about popular customs frees us from
what, and with what goal in view?

CHAPTER 17

How to Pray and Be Heard by God

THE Bible says of Jehovah God: "O Hearer of prayer, even to you people of all flesh will come." (Psalm 65:2 [64:3, *Dy*]) Yes, God does hear prayers. And persons in all the earth who love the truth, who long to do his will, and who approach him in the way he approves, can enjoy this precious privilege. (Acts 10:34, 35) Really, what a marvelous privilege it is to be able to talk to the glorious Ruler of all the universe and know that he hears you!—Psalm 8:1, 3, 4 [8:2, 4, 5, *Dy*]; Isaiah 45:22.

[2] Encouragingly, his written Word promises: "Do not be anxious over anything, but in everything by prayer and supplication along with thanksgiving let your petitions be made known to God; and the peace of God that excels all thought will guard your hearts and your mental powers by means of Christ Jesus." (Philippians 4:6, 7) However, some may personally feel uncertain about the matter of prayer because many of their prayers seem to have gone unanswered. Why is this? It is important for us to know. In his Word, God makes clear what his will is regarding prayer.

---

1. What does Psalm 65:2 say about God, and who may come to him with assurance of being heard?

2. (a) With regard to prayer, what promise does the Bible give at Philippians 4:6, 7? (b) Why do some feel uncertainty about prayer?

THE WAY OF APPROACH TO GOD IN PRAYER

³ The Bible tells us that "he that approaches
God must believe that he is and that he becomes
the rewarder of those earnestly seeking him."
(Hebrews 11:6) Notice that this scripture says
we are to 'approach God.' As the true and living
God, Jehovah wants us to pray to him, not to
someone else. Prayer is part of our worship and
for this reason should be directed only to the
Creator, Jehovah. (Matthew 4:10) Jesus Christ
taught his followers to pray to his "Father in the
heavens." (Matthew 6:9) Jesus did not teach them
to pray to himself, nor to his human mother Mary,
nor to any other person. Jehovah is all-powerful,
all-wise, perfect in justice and in love. So, why
should we go to any lesser person? Further, the
inspired apostle Paul assures us that God "is not
far off from each one of us," if we seek him in
the right way.—Acts 17:27.

⁴ But you may say, "How can we, as imperfect
creatures with inherited sin, pray to a God who is
perfect and righteous?" Jehovah has lovingly
taken this into consideration and provided a "helper" to speak for us in heaven. That helper is "Jesus
Christ, a righteous one." (1 John 2:1, 2) He gave
his life as a ransom for mankind. Moreover, Jehovah has appointed him as his High Priest. Jehovah requires us to recognize the position of his
Son in His purpose and to offer all our prayers
in his name. That is why Jesus told his followers:
"No one comes to the Father except through me."
(John 14:6) Jesus also said: "If you ask the
Father for anything he will give it to you in my
name." (John 16:23) For our prayers to be accept-

3. To whom should all our prayers be directed, and why?
4. For our prayers to be acceptable to God, in whose name
should they be offered? Why?

able to God, then, we must pray to Jehovah God through his Son, that is, in the name of Jesus.

PRAYERS THAT ARE PLEASING TO GOD

[5] At 1 Peter 3:12 we read: "The eyes of Jehovah are upon the righteous ones, and his ears are toward their supplication." Thus, if our prayers are to please God, we must be sincere in trying to live our lives in harmony with the righteous principles of God's Word. If one rejects God's Word and his will he should not expect God to answer his prayers for help in time of trouble. (Proverbs 15:29; 28:9) For example, to those who do not respect the sacredness of life, God says: "Even though you make many prayers, I am not listening; with bloodshed your very hands have become filled." (Isaiah 1:15) In this "time of the end" when violence, immorality, dishonesty, false worship and other wrong conduct are becoming more and more common, we certainly need to consider seriously the way we live our daily lives if we want our prayers to be heard by God. —1 John 3:21, 22.

[6] What we pray for also has much to do with determining whether God will answer our prayers. Jesus gave his disciples a model prayer to guide them as to the kind of prayer God accepts. (Matthew 6:9-13) This prayer shows that God's name and purposes should be our first concern. Next, we may ask for our material needs, for forgiveness and for deliverance from temptation and from the

---

5. (a) In view of what 1 Peter 3:12 says, how should we sincerely try to live our lives if our prayers are to be heard by God? (b) Who should not expect God to hear his prayers for help?

6. (a) According to Jesus' instructions, what should be the matter of first concern in our prayers? (b) How did Jesus show that our prayers should be not just for ourselves? For whom, then, should we pray?

wicked one. Note, too, that Jesus teaches us to pray to "*our* Father" to "give *us* today our bread" and to "forgive *us*." This shows that, when praying, a person should think not just of himself, or of his own problems and needs. Instead he should unselfishly broaden out his prayers to include others. We should include, not only our own family and relatives, but others who are seeking to please God, and especially those who face trials and difficulties in their service to God.—James 5:16; Ephesians 6:18-20.

⁷ The apostle John writes: "This is the confidence that we have toward him, that, no matter what it is that we ask according to his will, he hears us." (1 John 5:14) Yes, every part of a Christian's life is a proper matter for prayer. But the important thing is that what he requests be in harmony with God's will. This is a foremost reason why many prayers go unanswered. The person has not tried first to find out what God's will is. (Proverbs 3:5-7) So, rather than deciding what *we* want to do or have, and praying to God about it, is it not proper to find out first what God wants of us, what is his will for us, and then frame our prayers accordingly?—James 4:3, 13-15.

⁸ By our study of God's Word and by our experience in serving him in association with other true Christians we can come to understand his will. (Romans 12:2) The psalmist prayed: "Make me understand, that I may observe your law and that I may keep it with the whole heart. Cause me to tread in the pathway of your commandments, for in it I have taken delight. Incline my

---

7. (a) What is a foremost reason why many prayers are not answered? (b) To offer acceptable prayers, what should we do first?
8. (a) How can we come to understand God's will? (b) Will God really give us the wisdom to guide our course in life?

heart to your reminders, and not to profits."
(Psalm 119:34-36 [118:34-36, *Dy*]) If we pray
to God in faith, he will generously give us the
wisdom we need to cope with the problems of life.
(James 1:5-8) He will help us to know and do
what will bring honor to his own great name, and
this will result also in our own happiness.—Psalm
84:11, 12 [83:12, 13, *Dy*].

THE PROPER MANNER OF PRAYING

⁹ Does God require that we assume a certain
position when praying or that we go to a particular
building to pray? His Word shows that he does
not. (Nehemiah 8:6;* Daniel 6:10; Mark 11:25;
John 11:41) Jesus indicated that it is good to have
privacy in personal prayer, going into one's own
room to pray. (Matthew 6:6) And though Jesus
himself prayed at times in public places, he strongly condemned praying before others just to be
seen by them and to make a show of one's "holi-
ness." He also showed that God does not approve
of using the very same words over and over again
in prayer. (Matthew 6:5, 7, 8) Why is this?

¹⁰ It is because what really matters to God is
what is in our heart. "For, as regards Jehovah, his
eyes are roving about through all the earth to
show his strength in behalf of those whose heart
is complete toward him." (2 Chronicles 16:9)†
How could our prayer express what is in our heart
if it is simply read out of a prayer book? So, when
we pray, we should do so from the heart, with
humility. "God opposes the haughty ones, but he

* 2 Esdras 8:6, *Dy*.
† 2 Paralipomenon 16:9, *Dy*.

9. (a) When we pray, is any certain position required?
(b) What did Jesus show about personal prayer? (c) What
kind of praying did Jesus condemn?
10. (a) Explain why our prayers should not be read out of a
book. (b) What kind of language should we use when we pray?

gives undeserved kindness to the humble ones."
(James 4:6) In our prayers there is no value in
using language that is unusual or high-sounding.
Rather, we should talk to God as we would to a
close and trusted friend and as a son to his father.
Our prayer may even be a silent one, in our own
heart. (1 Samuel 1:12, 13)* At times we may not
find just the right words to express our thoughts
to God. But we can be confident that God knows
our needs and will understand our simple prayer.

APPRECIATING THE PRIVILEGE OF PRAYER

[11] We all reach times in our lives when no human
help is available or when the help humans offer
is not sufficient for our needs. Then it is to God
alone that we must turn. However, if we love Jehovah and appreciate the privilege of prayer we
certainly will not wait for such occasions to speak
to him. Instead, we will approach him regularly,
frequently, with expressions of thanksgiving and
praise, as well as with our petitions and requests.
(Ephesians 6:18; 1 Thessalonians 5:17, 18) A
family benefits greatly from prayer, even the
simple expression of thanks to God at mealtimes,
following the example of Jesus.—Matthew 14:19.

[12] Truly, private prayer, family prayer and congregational prayer all bring marvelous benefits.
Prayer shows a frank recognition of our complete
dependence on God for everything. It draws us
close to fellow worshipers. It brings upon us the
peace of the loving Creator. It promotes the flow
of God's holy spirit in our lives. It helps us to be
confident about the future. It is a gift from God
and one that we should appreciate and use.

---

* 1 Kings 1:12, 13, Dy.

11. (a) Should we wait till we need special help before praying
to God? (b) Why is prayer appropriate at mealtimes?
12. State some of the marvelous benefits of prayer?

CHAPTER 18

Christian Obedience to Law

LAWLESSNESS is widespread in the world today, but those who truly live in harmony with the Bible do not contribute to it. They take to heart the counsel of God's Word, which says: "Be obedient to governments and authorities as rulers."—Titus 3:1.

² It is true that some who now practice true worship previously did engage in lawless conduct. They may have stolen things that belonged to others. Perhaps they viewed obedience to certain laws as important only when the police were in sight. In this they were probably no worse than many others in the community. However, the Bible made clear to them that, if they were going to take up true worship, they would need a very different outlook on life.—Ephesians 4:22-29.

³ Commenting on the attitude that a Christian should have toward the political governments, the apostle Paul said: "Let every soul be in subjection to the superior authorities, for there is no authority except by God." (Romans 13:1) This does not mean that God established these governments

---

1. Though lawlessness is widespread, what course do those who conform to the Bible follow?
2. What attitude toward law must true worshipers leave behind?
3. (a) What should a Christian's attitude toward political governments be? (b) Why should a Christian not join in riots or in civil disobedience to interfere with government activity?

or that he approves of their course. Some of them plainly say that they are atheistic. Nonetheless, God permits them to exist. They would not be able to exercise authority at all if God did not allow it. (John 19:11) And if God permits them to rule, why should any Christian interfere with their doing so? Even if a person disagrees with what the government is doing, why should he join in a riot or share in civil disobedience to try to prevent the State from carrying on its business? Anyone doing so will get himself into trouble, not only with the secular government, but also with God. As Romans 13:2 says: "Therefore he who opposes the authority has taken a stand against the arrangement of God; those who have taken a stand against it will receive judgment to themselves."

⁴ It is a good thing to show proper respect for the government and appreciation for the beneficial services that it performs. We all have good reason to be glad that the governments under which we live provide roads for travel, schools for education, fire protection and food inspection. Courts of law and protection against crime are also of great value. In these and other matters the "superior authorities" show themselves to be "God's public servants," providing services that benefit his people. So when we are asked to pay for all these public services by means of taxes, we do well to call to mind the scripture that says: "There is therefore compelling reason for you people to be in subjection, not only on account of that wrath [in punishment of law violators] but also on account of your conscience. For that is why you are also paying taxes; for they are God's

4. (a) What benefits do governments provide for us? (b) What view should Christians have regarding the paying of taxes?

public servants constantly serving this very purpose. Render to all their dues, to him who calls for the tax, the tax; to him who calls for the tribute, the tribute."—Romans 13:5-7.

⁵ But how far does this subjection to political authorities go? Is it unlimited? Is obedience to human law even more important than obedience to the law of God? Certainly not! Notice that in the scripture just quoted the "compelling reason" for obedience is said to include "your conscience." So, one's conscience is not to be ignored, especially if that conscience has been trained by the Word of God. Jesus Christ showed that there are two aspects to consider. Pointing out that it was proper to pay tax to the Roman State, he said, "Pay back Caesar's things to Caesar," and then he added: "But God's things to God." (Mark 12:17) So it is vital for each one of us to examine his course of life to be certain that, above all, he is not contributing to the widespread disregard for the law of God.—Psalm 1:1-3.

OBEDIENCE TO THE SUPREME LAW

⁶ Not long after the death of Jesus Christ, his apostles were called on to show where they stood on this matter. They were ordered by the rulers in Jerusalem to stop preaching in the name of Jesus Christ. Did they comply? Would you have done so? The apostles firmly replied: "We must obey God as ruler rather than men." (Acts 5:29; see also 4:18-20.) They did not treat lightly their obligations before the law of the land, but when a direct conflict arose between man's law and the law of God, they recognized that God's law is

5. (a) Is Christian obedience to political authorities unlimited?
(b) How did Jesus show there are two aspects to consider?
6. What did the apostles do when they were ordered to stop preaching? So whose law did they obey as supreme?

supreme. Seeing this, a respected member of the
court before which they appeared wisely counseled
his fellow judges not to interfere with these Christians, so that they as officials would not become
fighters against God.—Acts 5:33-39.

⁷ It is not only God's commandments about
preaching that are important. There are other
matters too. Highlighting one of them, Jehovah
said to his people in the days of Moses: "You
must not make for yourself a carved image or
a form like anything that is in the heavens above
or that is on the earth underneath or that is in
the waters under the earth. You must not bow
down to them nor be induced to serve them, because I Jehovah your God am a God exacting exclusive devotion." (Exodus 20:4, 5) Nevertheless,
many objects of devotion have been made by men.
Some of them have been made of metal or wood.
Others have been made of cloth, with a form representing some object in heaven or on earth sewed
or painted onto them. In some cases the acts of
devotion performed before these have been volun-
tary, but in other cases they have been required
by secular law. Does this make a difference? If
the secular law requires certain acts of devotion
to be performed before an image or emblem, does
this relieve individuals of the obligation to obey
God's law on the matter? Faithful worshipers of
Jehovah in the district of Babylon did not believe
so. The Bible tells us that three young Hebrews,
Shadrach, Meshach and Abednego, refused to
participate in a ceremony ordered by the king.
Why? Because it involved worship, and their

7. (a) What did God say in the days of Moses about performing
an act of devotion before an image? (b) What kind of objects
of devotion have men made? (c) When secular law requires
acts of devotion before an image or emblem, whose example
do Christians do well to consider?

worship belonged only to Jehovah. God approved of what they did. But how did the king of Babylon react? At first he was violently angry. Yet, in time, he saw the hand of Jehovah God in the matter. Realizing that they were no danger to the State, he issued a decree protecting their freedom. (Daniel 3:1-30) Do you not admire their loyalty to God? Do you not want to be just as firm as they were in giving worship exclusively to God?

⁸ This same issue of worship confronted Christians living in the Roman Empire. The State required that everyone burn incense to the emperor as an evidence of loyalty. This the Christians could not do, although they obeyed the other laws. They realized that worship was involved, whether the act was performed in honor of an emblem or of a person. (Matthew 4:10) Justin Martyr, who lived in the second century, expressed the views of these Christians, saying: "God alone we render worship, but in other things we gladly serve you [the political rulers], acknowledging you as kings and rulers of men." These Christians were often misunderstood, but what they did really showed no disrespect, did it? Nor did it make them a danger to other Romans. As the Roman governor Pliny the Younger reported in a letter to Emperor Trajan, they refused to commit fraud or theft or adultery. They were the kind of people that anyone would like to have as neighbors, and it was their religion that made them that way.

⁹ In addition to our worship, there is something else that we owe to God. An apostle of Jesus Christ pointed to this when he said: "The God that made

---

8. (a) What did the Roman State require of its subjects, and why did the early Christians refuse? (b) Were these Christians showing disrespect?
9. Besides our worship, what else do we owe God?

the world and all the things in it . . . gives to all persons life." (Acts 17:24, 25) None of us would be alive if it were not for God. He is the Source of life. (Psalm 36:9 [35:10, *Dy*]) But what are we doing with the life that he permits us to enjoy?

¹⁰ True Christians recognize that, to enjoy God's approval, they must avoid using their lives in activities that will put them in opposition to God. So they avoid the course of those classes of persons whom the Bible describes as being in line for destruction by God's executioner when this wicked system ends. (Revelation 19:17-21) They appreciate that Jehovah's judgment is true and righteous. And they mold their lives now in harmony with his will. They are well aware that this may bring upon them disapproval, even persecution, from those whose only interests lie in this present system of things. But, with full faith that God's way is right, they exalt his law and his worship, giving these first place in their lives. (Micah 4: 1-3) In imitation of God's own Son, Jesus Christ, they use their lives, not for selfish pursuits nor for the will of selfish men, but in harmony with the will of God. (1 Corinthians 7:23; 1 Peter 4: 1, 2) So doing, they truly pay back to God what belongs to him.   —

¹¹ Do you want to have God's approval? If so, obedience to law will be a serious matter in your life. It will move you to have due regard for the person and property of your neighbors. It will make you respectful toward government officials. But, above all, it will cause you to bring your life into full harmony with the judicial decisions of Jehovah God, the greatest Lawgiver of all.

---

10. How do the Scriptures help us to avoid displeasing God by the way we use our lives?
11. How should obedience to law affect our lives?

CHAPTER 19

Godly Respect for Life and Blood

HOW much safer we would be if everyone had godly respect for life and blood! But many persons do not have such respect. Violence and bloodshed are on the increase everywhere. In many places a person's life is in danger if he simply walks the streets alone at night. So accustomed has the world become to violence that, even for entertainment, people will sit for hours and watch it on television or in a motion picture. However, the Bible teaches us that life is something sacred. Do you view it that way?

² Unscriptural attitudes have become so commonplace today that Bible teachings on the matter may surprise some persons at first. However, the Author of the Bible, who is also the Giver of life and the Creator of blood, is the Supreme Authority on the subject. His laws are to be respected. —Psalm 36:5-9 [35:6-10, *Dy*]; Isaiah 55:8, 9.

"SHEDDING MAN'S BLOOD"

³ It was first to Cain, a son of Adam, that Jehovah spoke about the seriousness of taking human

1. Though the world is accustomed to violence, how does the Bible teach us to view life?
2. Why may Bible teachings on life and blood surprise some persons?
3. (a) To whom did God first speak about the seriousness of taking human life? Why? (b) After the Flood, how did God emphasize the preciousness of life? (c) Is that law out-of-date?

life. God had already warned Cain that his anger might lead him into sin, but Cain ignored the warning and assaulted his brother Abel, killing him. Then God said: "Listen! Your brother's blood is crying out to me from the ground." For his lawless shedding of blood Cain had to answer to God. (Genesis 4:6-11) Following the flood of Noah's day, God again emphasized that human life is precious in his sight. "Your blood of your souls shall I ask back," God said. "Anyone shedding man's blood, by man will his own blood be shed, for in God's image he made man." (Genesis 9:5, 6) That commandment has not gone out-of-date. It applies to all mankind today as descendants of Noah. Whether human governments deal with criminals in accord with that divine law or not, Jehovah will call to account those who lawlessly take life.

⁴ To remain blameless before the Giver of life, however, there is more required. At 1 John 3:15 it is written: "Everyone who hates his brother is a manslayer, and you know that no manslayer has everlasting life remaining in him." If we want everlasting life, we need to root out of our lives all hatred for our fellowmen. God is not going to preserve into his new system persons who, like Cain, ignore divine warning and endanger the lives of others with their hot tempers. A godly view of life requires that we learn to love our fellowman.—1 John 3:11, 12; Matthew 5:21, 22.

⁵ If we conform to God's thinking on this matter, we will also appreciate that life is no less sacred because a person may be very old or very young. God's Word shows that even the life of an

4. If we want eternal life, what must we root out of our lives, so as not to endanger the lives of others?
5. What is the Scriptural view toward abortion?

unborn child in its mother's womb is precious to Jehovah. (Exodus 21:22, 23; Psalm 127:3 [126:3, *Dy*]) And yet millions of abortions are performed throughout the earth each year. These are a violation of God's law, for the human embryo is a living creature and should not be destroyed. If married couples want to limit the size of their families for economic, health or other reasons, that is their personal affair, and the way in which they do this is largely a matter for them to work out personally. But we must face the fact that the practice of abortion does not show a godly respect for life.

'KEEP YOURSELVES FREE FROM BLOOD'

[6] The holy Bible frequently uses "blood" to stand for "life." This is because the life or soul is in the blood. (Leviticus 17:11) Since God is the Creator of blood, he knows more about it than any of us, and he has the full right to say what may be done with it. It was first after the global Flood that God granted humankind permission to eat animal flesh. So at that time he also gave them his law on blood, saying: "Every moving animal that is alive may serve as food for you. As in the case of green vegetation, I do give it all to you. Only flesh with its soul—its blood—you must not eat." (Genesis 9:3, 4) Animal flesh might be eaten, but not the blood.

[7] Later, that law was embodied in the commandments given to the nation of Israel, and God's Word makes it binding on Christians as well. After

---

6. (a) Who has the full right to say what may be done with blood? (b) When God granted man permission to eat animal food, what law did he give on blood?
7. (a) What did the governing body of the early Christians write about blood? (b) How does that decision indicate the seriousness of 'keeping free from blood'?

thoroughly discussing God's requirements for
Christians, the governing body of the early Christian congregation wrote to the non-Jewish believers: "The holy spirit and we ourselves have fa-
vored adding no further burden to you, except
these necessary things, to keep yourselves free
from things sacrificed to idols and from blood and
from things strangled and from fornication. If
you carefully keep yourselves from these things,
you will prosper. Good health to you!" (Acts 15:
28, 29) So, we, too, must 'keep free from blood.'
And our doing so is a serious matter, having been
put on a level with avoiding fornication and
idolatry.

⁸ It is evident from what God says about blood
that we should not eat the flesh of an animal that
has not been bled. (Deuteronomy 12:15, 16) Nor
should we consume animal blood by itself or mixed
in other foods. But is it only the blood of animals
that is involved? Certainly God did not forbid
mankind to eat animal blood while permitting him
to eat human blood, as if it were less sacred! He
made this clear when he later said to the Israelites: "As for any man . . . who eats *any sort of
blood,* I shall certainly set my face against the soul
that is eating the blood."—Leviticus 17:10.

⁹ This was well understood by the early Christians. Even though it was commonly believed that
drinking the blood of another human would benefit one's health, they knew that lasting good
health, both physical and spiritual, depended upon
obedience to God. So, Tertullian, a Christian writ-

8. (a) If an animal has not been bled, should its flesh be
eaten? (b) Should blood be mixed in any kind of food?
(c) Why is human blood not less sacred?
9. What did an early Christian writer say about (a) the reason
why some drank blood at that time? (b) the view of the early
Christians regarding blood?

er of the second and third centuries C.E., said: "Those, too, who at the gladiator shows, for the cure of epilepsy, quaff with greedy thirst the blood of criminals slain in the arena, as it flows fresh from the wound, and then rush off—to whom do they belong? . . . Blush for your vile ways before the Christians, who have not even the blood of animals at their meals of simple and natural foods; who abstain from things strangled and that die a natural death. . . . To clench the matter with a single example, you tempt Christians with sausages of blood, just because you are perfectly aware that the thing by which you thus try to get them to transgress they hold unlawful." They understood God's law to include blood of every kind, animal and human.

[10] What about the use to which human blood is put today? Medical doctors, realizing the life-sustaining power of blood, use blood transfusions freely in their treatment of patients. Is this in harmony with God's will? Some persons may reason that getting a blood transfusion is not actually "eating." But is it not true that when a patient is unable to eat through his mouth, doctors often feed him by the same method in which a blood transfusion is administered? Examine the scriptures carefully and notice that they tell us to '*keep free* from blood' and to '*abstain* from blood.' (Acts 15:20, 29) What does this mean? If a doctor were to tell you to abstain from alcohol, would that mean simply that you should not take it through your mouth but that you could transfuse it directly into your veins? Of course not!

10. (a) Explain why getting a blood transfusion is not actually different from "eating." (b) Illustrate that 'abstaining from blood' means not taking it into our bodies at all.

So, too, 'abstaining from blood' means not taking it into our bodies at all.

[11] Does this put God's servants at a disadvantage in comparison with persons who ignore the Bible and take blood transfusions? No, it works no real hardship on them. Do not forget that, immediately after telling Christians to 'keep themselves from blood,' the Scripture says: "If you carefully keep yourselves from these things, you will prosper. Good health to you!" (Acts 15:29) God had that recorded in the Bible for a purpose. He knows what he is talking about! He knows more about blood than do doctors whose efforts, though they may be well meaning, do not always produce the desired results. (Mark 5:25-29) The fact is that, while most patients survive blood transfusions, many become diseased as a result of them and thousands die every year as a direct result of them. There are other forms of treatment that do not cause such harm. A doctor may tell a person that he will be dead within a short time if he does not submit to a transfusion, but the patient may die even though he accepts blood. On the other hand, as you know, there are many patients who regain good health in spite of a doctor's predictions to the contrary.

[12] For the doubtful chance that one might be kept alive for a few more years in this system of things, would it make good sense to turn one's back on God by breaking his law? If we try to save our life, or soul, by breaking God's law, we

---

11. (a) Does 'abstaining from blood' work any real hardship on God's servants? (b) What happens to many patients who get blood transfusions? (c) Can doctors be sure that a person will die if he is not given blood?
12. (a) Why is it not wise to try to save one's life by breaking God's law? (b) Is our present life more precious than loyalty to God?

will lose it everlastingly. That is why Jesus said: "Whoever wants to save his soul will lose it; but whoever loses his soul for my sake will find it." (Matthew 16:25) So the wise course is always to have confidence in the rightness of God's law and full faith that, if need be, God can give us life again by a resurrection in his new system of things. (1 Thessalonians 4:13, 14) In that way we will show godly respect for life. We will not view our present life as being more precious than loyalty to God. Instead, we will keep our eye on God's provision of *eternal* life for those who walk in the way of the truth.

[13] As never before, there is an urgent need for people everywhere to get God's viewpoint of life. They need to learn of the provision that Jehovah God himself has made to save life. He sent his Son Jesus Christ to shed his own lifeblood on behalf of those who will exercise faith, and he resurrected him from the dead. (Hebrews 13:20, 21) It is not by blood transfusions but only by means of faith in Jesus' shed blood that salvation can be had. And it is urgent to gain and exercise that faith now before this old system of things comes to its end. If we have learned about this loving provision, then we should feel moved to tell others about it. Godly concern for the lives of other people will move us to do it with zeal and boldness. (Ezekiel 3:17-21) If we shoulder this responsibility and persist in it until they have all had opportunity to hear, we will be able to say, as did the apostle Paul: "I am clean from the blood of all men, for I have not held back from telling you all the counsel of God."—Acts 20:26, 27.

---

13. (a) Rather than by blood transfusions, how only can salvation be had? (b) What do we need to do in order to be "clean from the blood of all men," as the apostle Paul was?

CHAPTER 20

Building a Happy Family Life

IN ADDITION to providing the truth on doctrinal matters, the Bible also gives much sound counsel concerning home life. It shows us how to cope successfully with the problems of everyday life. There is no place where we could find better advice, because Jehovah, the Author of the Bible, is also the One who originated marriage and arranged for family life.—Genesis 2:18, 22.

² When God brought the first man and woman together as husband and wife, he emphasized the unity that should exist between them. Jesus Christ drew attention to this when he said: "Did you not read that he who created them from the beginning made them male and female and said, 'For this reason a man will leave his father and his mother and will stick to his wife, and the two will be one flesh'? So that they are no longer two, but one flesh." (Matthew 19:4-6) They were not to be competitors. Nor were they simply to be acquaintances that shared the same dwelling place. No, they were to be "one flesh." So, marriage mates should cultivate deep love for each other, and seek to be drawn together in unity of purpose.

---

1. Why is there no better place than the Bible to get advice about home life?
2. (a) How did Jesus Christ draw attention to the unity that should exist between husband and wife? (b) What does this require that they cultivate?

RELATIONSHIP OF HUSBAND AND WIFE

[3] For married life really to be happy, both husband and wife must appreciate their respective positions. These are not set merely by local custom. They are outlined in God's own Word the Bible, and are in harmony with the qualities that God implanted in man and woman at the time of creation. Knowing how he made man, and the purpose he had in view, Jehovah recorded in his Word that "a husband is head of his wife as the Christ also is head of the congregation." (Ephesians 5:23) This means that the husband is to take the lead in the home, planning family activities and shouldering the responsibility for making final decisions. But this does not authorize him to be a harsh or cruel ruler of his household. —Colossians 3:19.

[4] Though many men have exercised headship in an unloving way, Christian husbands should avoid this. They should study carefully how Jesus Christ has exercised headship over the Christian congregation, and then follow his fine example. At Ephesians 5:25 husbands are counseled: "Continue loving your wives, just as the Christ also loved the congregation and delivered up himself for it." So doing, they will not be overly demanding of their wives, but will handle family affairs in a way that refreshes everyone concerned. —Matthew 11:28-30.

[5] The wife, for her part, "should have deep respect for her husband." (Ephesians 5:33) Since

3. (a) How does Ephesians 5:23 describe the position of the husband? (b) What does this mean?
4. Whose fine example should Christian husbands study, and with what benefits?
5. (a) How should a Christian wife view her husband? (b) If a wife is keener of mind than her husband, how can she use this quality in a beneficial way? (c) What responsibilities of married women are set out at Titus 2:4, 5?

he is the one authorized by God to take the lead, she can make a great contribution to family happiness by willingly submitting to his headship. (Colossians 3:18) If she is keener of mind than her husband, as is sometimes the case, then she can use this quality to support him in his role as head, rather than competing with him or belittling what he does. (Proverbs 12:4) There is much for her to do in connection with family life. The Bible fittingly urges married women "to love their husbands, to love their children, to be sound in mind, chaste, workers at home, good, subjecting themselves to their own husbands, so that the word of God may not be spoken of abusively." (Titus 2:4, 5) The wife and mother who fulfills these duties will win the lasting love and respect of her family.—Proverbs 31:10, 11, 26-28.

⁶ In many homes problems arise when a husband fails to take into consideration the womanly temperament, the emotional makeup, of his wife. He needs to appreciate that she views things differently. Her emotions respond in a different way. Her strength is not the same as his. Thus the inspired advice to husbands is: "Continue dwelling . . . with them according to knowledge, assigning them honor as to a weaker vessel, the feminine one, since you are also heirs with them of the undeserved favor of life." (1 Peter 3:7) When a husband does this, he helps to bring about a spirit of understanding and security in the home.

⁷ It is common among worldly people for the security of the home to be undermined by sex

6. (a) What do some husbands fail to consider with regard to their wives, thus giving rise to problems? (b) So what does 1 Peter 3:7 advise husbands to do?
7. (a) How does applying what is written at Hebrews 13:4 contribute to a sense of security in the home? (b) To whom must a Christian's sex interests be limited, and why?

interests outside the marriage bond. But those who live in harmony with God's Word are protected against the heartache and grief that such conduct brings. In language that is easy to understand the Bible warns: "Let marriage be honorable among all, and the marriage bed be without defilement, for God will judge fornicators and adulterers." (Hebrews 13:4) There is no allowance for immoral conduct. Those who want to be servants of God must lead clean lives. (1 Thessalonians 4:3-8) They must limit their sex interests to their own legal marriage mates, and they are accountable before God to do so. (Proverbs 5:15-21) It ought to be the earnest desire of both husband and wife to help each other to avoid any temptation to wrongdoing. They can do this by showing unselfish consideration for each other. —1 Corinthians 7:3-5.

[8] However, if a marriage union is truly going to function in harmony with the godly principles that we have discussed, there must also be regular emphasis on spiritual matters. The worship of Jehovah God should be of first importance in the home. It should not be shoved aside in favor of efforts to obtain more material possessions or to have more time for the pursuit of pleasure. (Luke 8:11, 14, 15) Family prayer and regular sessions of family Bible study should be part of every family's way of life. Do you arrange for this in your home?

REARING CHILDREN IN A GODLY WAY

[9] When children are born, it is the earnest desire of loving parents to see that the lives of those

8. (a) For a marriage to work well, what must be of first importance in the home? (b) So what should be part of the family's way of life?
9. How can problems in rearing children be met successfully?

young ones turn out well. But the task is not an easy one. There are many problems that arise along the way. These can be met successfully only by applying the counsel in God's Word.—Proverbs 22:6; Deuteronomy 11:18-21.

[10] Much time and effort are usually required to see that there are proper food, clean clothing and a pleasant home in which to live. But the Bible repeatedly shows that the responsibility of parents by no means ends there. It is also vital to include the children regularly in the family's program of instruction in the Word of God. (Psalm 78:5-7 [77:5-7, *Dy*]) Not only during regular study sessions, but at other times too parents should talk to their children about Jehovah and his ways. (Deuteronomy 6:6, 7) When this is done, children learn to think of God in relationship to all the activities of life.

[11] It is principally on the father, as head of the household, that the Scriptures lay the responsibility to see that this instruction is given. When he makes provision for it and personally takes the lead in giving it, the entire family is drawn more closely together. At the same time, the children are given the kind of training that they so greatly need. So it is important to take to heart what is recorded at Ephesians 6:4: "You, fathers, do not be irritating your children, but go on bringing them up in the discipline and authoritative advice of Jehovah."—See also Proverbs 4:1.

[12] Part of the "discipline . . . of Jehovah" that must be taught involves the child's obligation to

---

10. (a) What besides food, clothing and shelter do children vitally need? (b) When should this be provided?
11. Who has the principal responsibility to see that children are given instruction in God's Word, and how does the Bible show this?
12. Why is obedience to parents not to be treated lightly?

be obedient to its parents. This is not something to be treated lightly, because the child's prospects for eternal life are involved. (Ephesians 6:1-3) God is the one who requires that children obey their parents. It shows wisdom on the part of the parents if they patiently and consistently impress this lesson on the mind and heart of their offspring.—Colossians 3:20, 23.

[13] There will be times when this calls for more than just telling the child what is right. When he deliberately does what he knows to be wrong, stronger action is required to impress the seriousness of the matter on him. Wisely the Bible observes: "Foolishness is tied up with the heart of a boy; the rod of discipline is what will remove it far from him." (Proverbs 22:15) Due to inherited imperfection children are born with a tendency to do what is bad, so they need correction. A loving parent will not neglect this. As Proverbs 13:24 says: "The one holding back his rod is hating his son, but the one loving him is he that does look for him with discipline."

[14] Discipline that is administered in love has the lasting good of the child in view. It is not done in violent bursts of anger or with loud screaming of threats. That is not the Christian way. (Ephesians 4:31, 32) There must be firmness, but soundness of mind should also prevail. The parents themselves should be setting a good example, not just to put on an appearance of righteousness —children quickly see through that—but honestly, sincerely. And if they do so, the children will be

---

13. How does the Bible book of Proverbs stress the need to correct children when they deliberately do what is wrong?
14. How should discipline be administered in a Christian home, and with what good results?

helped to realize that God's righteous principles rule the household, and not just unreasonable whims or temporary moods. The young ones will not fear that they will be the victims of unjust punishment. Rather, they will associate punishment with the breaking of proper rules of good conduct.

[15] Among the righteous principles from the Bible that deserve serious family discussion are those having to do with godly moral standards. Children need to be taught, for example, that "everyone liking and carrying on a lie" is detestable to Jehovah. (Revelation 22:15; Proverbs 6: 16-19) Theft, too, in all its various forms, should be seen as a violation of God's moral standard. (Ephesians 4:28; Romans 13:9, 10) These young folks need to be warned, in a way that they will understand, against sexual immorality and anything that may lead to it. (Ephesians 5:5; Prov-

---

15. (a) What should children be taught with regard to: Lies? Theft? Sexual immorality? (b) How can parents train their children so they will do what is right even when away from the parents?

Regular sessions of Bible study should be part of every family's way of life

erbs 5:3-14) Discuss together as a family the various problems that arise at home, at school and in play. Reason together on the scriptures that show the kind of conduct that is pleasing to God. In this way the children will learn to apply the Bible in their own lives. It will be a safeguard, so that even when children are away from their parents the admonition they have received will continue to guide them.—Proverbs 6:20-23.

[16] Careful thought also needs to be given to choice of companions. Associates deeply influence one's life. Wholesome companions have a good effect, but "bad associations spoil useful habits." (1 Corinthians 15:33) Time and again the Bible record illustrates this fact. (Genesis 34:1, 2; Numbers 25:1, 2) Children may not appreciate the seriousness of this, but parents should. So it is an evidence of wisdom on their part to keep a loving eye on their children's choice of companions. These companions include, not only those with whom the children play, but also those about whom they read and those that they watch in motion pictures and on television.—Philippians 4:8.

[17] For family life to be truly satisfying, however, more is needed than avoiding what is harmful. There should also be the enjoyment of doing wholesome things together as a family. The real joy of family life is lost when each one goes his own way without regard for the others. But when there is upbuilding family discussion, when plans are laid together and everyone works together to fulfill them, the family is drawn together in

16. (a) What does the Bible say as to the effect of bad companions? (b) So how can parents show wisdom with regard to their children's choice of companions?
17. What else will help to make family life truly satisfying?

unity. (Proverbs 15:22) This is not difficult when there is love in the home. And love is a normal thing among those who truly know God and have his spirit.—1 John 4:7, 8; Galatians 5:22, 23.

SETTLING FAMILY DIFFICULTIES

18 Even in homes that are normally happy, difficulties may arise at times. These are often due to human imperfection, or the pressures of the world in which we live. What should be done when friction develops between family members? The solution is not too hard to find if we remember that all of us are imperfect. It is not only outside the home but also within the family circle that we need to apply the inspired counsel: "Clothe yourselves with the tender affections of compassion, kindness, lowliness of mind, mildness, and longsuffering. Continue putting up with one another and forgiving one another freely if anyone has a cause for complaint against another. Even as Jehovah freely forgave you, so do you also. But, besides all these things, clothe yourselves with love, for it is a perfect bond of union."—Colossians 3:12-14; see also Proverbs 10:12; 19:11.

19 When a problem appears to be of a particularly serious nature, there are steps that can be taken to prepare the way for loving forgiveness. For example, when a dispute arises between the children, one of the parents might sit down with them, listen to the problem, and then encourage fitting apologies and the needed forgiveness. On these occasions scriptures such as the ones that we have just read could be reviewed with benefit.

18. How can the counsel at Colossians 3:12-14 help us to settle any family difficulties that may arise?
19. When a dispute arises between children, what might one of the parents do that would be really beneficial?

²⁰ When the difficulty is between husband and wife, it is certainly best not to air it before the children. Nor will the situation be improved by broadcasting complaints to friends and neighbors. Though one may have been deeply hurt, shouting will not make conditions any better. (Proverbs 29: 22) And the breach will only widen if the two go for days without talking to each other. The Christian thing to do is to discuss the problem together, with a firm resolve to restore peace. Even if the other person is the wrongdoer, make reconciliation easier by your own kindness. If you are at fault, humbly ask forgiveness. Do not postpone it; handle the problem without delay. "Let the sun not set with you in a provoked state." —Ephesians 4:26; see also Matthew 18:21-35.

²¹ Though divorce is common in the world, the Bible does not recommend it as the way to settle problems. Marriage is a lifelong tie, and is not to be regarded lightly. (Romans 7:2) God's Word allows only one ground on which a Christian may get a divorce that frees him for remarriage. What is that? It is adultery. In this event, it is up to the innocent one to decide whether to seek a divorce or not. (Matthew 5:32) However, divorce action should never be taken merely on suspicion; there ought to be clear-cut evidence.

²² In the past, before learning God's righteous requirements, some persons may have been hasty in getting a divorce, and now they have taken up

20. When some difficulty arises between husband and wife, what will not help in settling the matter, but what will?
21. (a) Is divorce the way to settle marriage problems? (b) What does the Bible say is the only ground for divorce that frees one for remarriage?
22. If one hastily got divorced before learning God's laws and has taken up living with another mate, what should he do if he wants to serve Jehovah?

living with another mate. What can they do about it? They cannot go back and live their lives over. But, if they want to have a part in the service of Jehovah God, and they are living with a mate, they should make sure that their present marriage is legally registered with the government. They ought to go to God in prayer and seek his forgiveness for their past course. Then they should work hard at living from this time on according to God's requirements on marriage.

²³ What if your marriage mate has declined to study God's Word with you? And what if you are not able to discuss problems together on the basis of Bible principles? The Bible still encourages you to stay together and not to view separation as the easy way out of your problems. Do what you personally can to improve the situation in your home by applying what the Bible says in regard to your own conduct. In time, because of your Christian conduct, you may win over your mate. (1 Corinthians 7:10-16; 1 Peter 3:1, 2) And what a blessing will be yours if your loving patience is rewarded in this way!

²⁴ There is much that can be done in every home in building toward a happier family life. Apply Bible counsel, and there will be good results! Let each one in the household lovingly seek the welfare of the others, thus strengthening family ties. (Colossians 3:14) Above all, share unitedly in true worship, so that all of you together will enjoy the rich blessing of Jehovah God, the One who can crown your happiness with eternal life.—Proverbs 3:11-18.

---

23. (a) Does the Bible encourage separation from an unbelieving mate when problems arise? (b) How can the believer improve the situation in the home, and with what possible result?
24. In summary, how can you build a happier family life?

CHAPTER 21

Your Decision to Serve God

THERE is so much for which to thank and praise Jehovah God. He has mercifully made provision for us to enjoy eternal life. Already he has arranged to erase the death-dealing effects of sin by providing his own Son as a ransom sacrifice. God's purpose to have his earthly children enjoy a paradise home forever will soon be realized! Does not this loving provision of God cause your heart to overflow with thankfulness to Him? —John 3:16; 1 John 4:9-11.

² True, none of us know everything about Jehovah and his ways. He is so great that humans will always be learning new things concerning him. (Romans 11:33) But on the basis of what you already know, have you not come to appreciate that everything he does is right and that there is every reason to put full confidence in him? Are you not convinced that he truly loves his creatures, that he is merciful and gracious, yet, at the same time, perfect in justice and wisdom? (Psalm 86: 5, 10, 15 [85:5, 10, 15, *Dy*]) If this is the way you feel about Jehovah God, you will be moved to serve Him, and nothing will hold you back.

---

1. What reasons do we have for giving thanks and praise to Jehovah God?
2. (a) On the basis of what you now know, what is your attitude toward Jehovah? (b) If we truly love Jehovah, what will we be moved to do?

³ Two courses are open to all humans. One leads to death and the other to eternal life. (Deuteronomy 30:19, 20) Which one will you take? Making the choice to serve Jehovah will lead to your greatest possible happiness, both now and forever. As the psalmist said: "Happy is the man in fear of Jehovah, in whose commandments he has taken very much delight."—Psalm 112:1 [111:1, *Dy*].

DEDICATION AND BAPTISM

⁴ When love for God moves you so that you want to do his will, then it is proper that you go to him in prayer through Jesus Christ and express your desire to be one of his servants, walking in the footsteps of his Son. It is appropriate that you tell Jehovah that you want to belong to him and that you want to do his will both now and for all time to come. (Psalm 104:33 [103:33, *Dy*]) In this way you dedicate yourself to God. This is a personal, private matter. No one else can do it for you.

⁵ After you have made your dedication to Jehovah to do his will, he will expect you to keep it. It is no light matter. Prove that you are a person of your word by faithfully sticking to this decision or dedication as long as you live. (Psalm 50:14 [49:14, *Dy*]) The Devil will use every possible means to make you break faith with Jehovah. But Jehovah himself will be with you. You can always turn to him in prayer, and he will support you. Also, as you have learned, God has an organization here on earth, and here you will

3. (a) What two courses are open to all persons? (b) What choice will lead to the greatest happiness?
4. When a person decides that he really wants to do God's will, what is it appropriate that he do?
5. (a) After you make your dedication to God, what does he expect you to do? (b) What help is available to you in living up to your dedication?

find mature Christians who will gladly give you loving encouragement and support.—1 Peter 5:8, 9; 3:12; 1 Thessalonians 5:11.

⁶ Deciding personally to serve Jehovah and expressing this determination in prayer is important. But there is something more. This was shown by Jesus Christ, who provided a pattern for us to follow. Remember, Jesus did more than just tell his Father that he had come to do His will. (Hebrews 10:7) When he began his service as a preacher of God's kingdom Jesus went to John the Baptist, at the Jordan River, and was baptized in water.—Matthew 3:13-15.

⁷ The Bible reveals that Jehovah God approved of Jesus' baptism. It says that, on that important occasion, "the heaven was opened up and the holy spirit in bodily shape like a dove came down upon him, and a voice came out of heaven: 'You are my Son, the beloved; I have approved you.'" (Luke 3:21, 22) Since Jesus set the pattern, dedicated Christians today also should be baptized. In fact, Jesus commanded his followers to make disciples of people of all nations and then to baptize these new disciples. This is no baptizing of infants. It is baptism of persons who have become *believers,* having made up their minds to serve Jehovah.—Matthew 28:19; Acts 8:12.

⁸ What, then, does Christian baptism signify? It is not a washing away of one's sins, because cleansing from sin comes only through faith in Jesus Christ. (Ephesians 1:7) Rather, it is a public demonstration, testifying that one has made

6. Why did Jesus go to John the Baptist at the Jordan River, and what do we learn from this?
7. (a) How does the Bible show that God approved of Jesus' baptism? (b) Why is the baptism commanded by Jesus not for infants?
8. Explain the significance of Christian baptism.

a solemn dedication to Jehovah God and is presenting himself to do His will. Thus, baptism is not to be viewed as of little importance. It is a requirement for all who obediently walk in the footsteps of Jesus Christ.

⁹ The Bible says that, after his baptism, Jesus "came up from the water." He had been actually down in the water so that John could completely immerse him. (Matthew 3:16; John 3:23) So, it was no mere sprinkling with water. Proper Christian baptism is accomplished by having a devoted servant of God—a male, as John the Baptist was—completely immerse the person in water and then raise him up again. If you have made up your mind to serve Jehovah and want to be baptized, then make this known to the overseer of the congregation of Jehovah's witnesses with which you are associated. He will gladly assist you, without any charge for the baptism.

THE CHRISTIAN MINISTRY

¹⁰ Of course, dedication and baptism are not the end of one's doing God's will. They are only the beginning. They mark the start of a happy life of serving Jehovah, with the prospect of continuing alive forever, doing his will. A dedicated Christian should always have the attitude of Jesus Christ, who said: "My food is for me to do the will of him that sent me and to finish his work." (John 4:34) A principal part of God's work for Jesus on earth was to preach the kingdom of God, and to lay the foundation for a preaching organization to carry on this activity after his death.

9. (a) In view of the way Jesus was baptized, how is proper Christian baptism accomplished? (b) If you want to be baptized, to whom in the congregation should you make this known?
10. (a) What attitude of Jesus should a Christian have? (b) When Jesus was on earth, what was God's will for him?

That was God's will for him, and Jesus faithfully did it.—Luke 4:43; John 17:4.

[11] What is God's will for Christians today? It is for them to do a similar preaching work, and one of great urgency. Bible prophecy reveals unmistakably that we are living now during "the conclusion of the system of things." And Jesus foretold regarding this time: "This good news of the kingdom will be preached in all the inhabited earth for a witness to all the nations; and then the end will come." (Matthew 24:3, 14) It is God's will that this preaching work be done now. The warning concerning the end of this wicked system must be sounded. Meek ones need to be shown the place of safety. Will you share in this work?—Zephaniah 2:2, 3;* Proverbs 24:11, 12.

[12] Jesus Christ set the example in performing the ministry. He preached everywhere, in the cities and villages, in homes and in public places —even to a woman at a wellside. (John 4:7, 21-24) A true Christian today will follow Jesus' example. He will preach at every opportunity. He will not simply wait for people to come to him, but he will endeavor to seek out persons with a listening ear. "Go," Jesus commanded, "make disciples of people of all the nations." (Matthew 28:19; see also 10:11-13.) This command applies to *all* Christians—laborers and housewives, elderly persons and youths—even as it did in the first century.—Acts 4:13; Romans 16:1.

[13] Early Christians followed Jesus' instruction

---

* Sophonias 2:2, 3, *Dy.*

11. (a) According to Jesus' words at Matthew 24:14, what is God's will for Christians today? (b) Why is this work urgent?
12. (a) How is the preaching work to be done? (b) Does Jesus' command to "make disciples" apply to all Christians?
13. Where is much of the preaching work done?

and example, making a special effort to call on people in their homes. (Luke 8:1; 10:1-6; Acts 5:42) The apostle Paul said: "I did not hold back from telling you any of the things that were profitable nor from teaching you publicly and from house to house." (Acts 20:20) This is still the principal way that true Christians carry on their ministry in our day.

[14] Those who share in this grand work do not do so in their own strength. Jehovah God backs them up. By his spirit he qualifies and empowers them for the ministry. (2 Corinthians 3:5, 6; 2 Timothy 4:17) Through his visible organization he provides training and assistance, at no financial cost, for all his witnesses. You, too, can enjoy the benefits of this provision, at your local Kingdom Hall.

[15] When you make your wholehearted decision to serve Jehovah God, you will experience rich blessings. The happiness that you have had in learning the truth about Jehovah and his purpose will be greatly enlarged as you share it with others and see the fine changes that it brings in their lives. (Acts 20:35; John 13:17) As you more fully apply God's Word in your own life you will be drawn closer to your Creator. You will enjoy his loving care in ways that you have never experienced before. (Revelation 7:9-17) Indeed, your wise course will make God's own heart rejoice. (Proverbs 27:11) And what joy will be yours as you experience fulfillment of the psalmist's words: "Happy is the people whose God is Jehovah!" —Psalm 144:15 [143:15, *Dy*].

---

14. How does God help us in the ministry?
15. When a person decides to serve God, what rich blessings are in store for him?

CHAPTER 22

True Worship
—a Way of Life

YOU have before you the prospect of life eternal under the kingdom of God. As you have seen, this prospect is solidly based in the truth of God's own Word. Its attainment is within your reach if you truly love God and worship him by "walking in the truth."—2 John 1-4.

² True worship means more than just knowing the truth. It means even more than speaking and proclaiming the truth to others. It means believing and acting on the truth, "walking in the truth" by putting it to work in our daily lives. (James 1: 22-25) True worship so influenced the daily lives of early Christians that it became known as "The Way" and "the way of the truth." (Acts 9:2; 2 Peter 2:2) It is the "way" marked out by God for all true worshipers to live their lives as they strive for the goal of eternal life.

³ So, our worship of Jehovah God cannot be something separate from the rest of our life. Rather, we must apply the truth of his Word in every activity of life. "Whether you are eating or drinking or doing anything else, do all things for

1. What prospect is now before us, but what must we do to lay hold of it?
2. By what term did true worship become known among the early Christians? Why?
3. Why must we apply the truth of God's Word in every activity of life?

187

God's glory." (1 Corinthians 10:31; see also Colossians 3:17.) Our every action should harmonize
with the truth of God's Word, and so bring glory
to God. This will be for our lasting happiness. The
righteous principles of his Word do not change
according to place of dwelling or personal circum-
stance. They are always true, always right.
—Psalm 119:142 [118:142, Dy].

⁴ If you really do practice true worship, what
will it mean for you now? It will bring your whole
life into harmony with God's way. His Word tells
us: "Put away the old personality which conforms
to your former course of conduct . . . you should
be made new in the force actuating your mind,
and should put on the new personality which was
created according to God's will in true righteousness and loyalty." (Ephesians 4:22-24) Putting on
the new personality means putting away obscene,
lying speech in favor of clean, truthful language.
It means replacing drunkenness and sexual immorality with upright, honorable conduct. It
means cultivating, not greediness, but unselfishness and generosity.—Colossians 3:5-10.

⁵ How refreshing it is when godly qualities are
displayed in one's everyday contacts with people
—with family members, business associates, close
acquaintances and strangers! (Colossians 3:12-
14, 18-23) But, do you think it difficult to make
this change, and maintain it every day? With the
help of God's spirit you can do it. Through true
worship you can produce the wonderful fruitage
of God's spirit in your life.—Galatians 5:19-24.

⁶ When true worship becomes your way of life

4. What is involved in putting on the new personality?
5. Is it possible to manifest godly qualities all the time? How?
6. (a) How does true worship affect one's making of decisions?
(b) Explain how true worship affects a Christian's employment
and his recreation.

it will be your constant guide. In making decisions, large or small, you will learn to ask yourself: "What will be pleasing to Jehovah God? What do the principles in his Word show to be the right and wise course?" (Psalm 119:105 [118:105, *Dy*]; Proverbs 3:1-6) For example, a true Christian will be concerned that his secular employment does not interfere with his service to Jehovah God, or involve work or practices that the Bible condemns. (Hebrews 13:5, 18; Isaiah 2:3, 4; Revelation 18:4) Even when it comes to recreation, God's Word should guide in selecting something upbuilding, wholesome. (Philippians 4:8) There is nothing in your life that will not be influenced in a beneficial way by true worship.

HAPPY REWARD FOR ENDURANCE

7 However, because of the pressures that the world brings upon genuine Christians, it may not be easy to continue walking faithfully in the "way of the truth." Jesus warned that true worshipers would be hated and persecuted, just as he was. (John 15:18-20; 2 Timothy 3:12) Circumstances may arise that threaten to interfere with your regular study of the Bible or your association with fellow Christians at congregational meetings. Opposition may cause the preaching work to become difficult, even dangerous. What will you do? The Bible counsels: "You have need of endurance, in order that, after you have done the will of God, you may receive the fulfillment of the promise." (Hebrews 10:36) So, the only right course is to press on courageously in God's service, trusting

---

7. (a) Why may it not be easy to continue walking in the "way of the truth"? (b) When faced with opposition, what is the right course, in view of Hebrews 10:36?

in Him to sustain you.—Psalm 55:22 [54:23, *Dy*];
Hebrews 6:11, 12.

⁸ To early Christians, the disciple James wrote:
"Consider it all joy, my brothers, when you meet
with various trials, knowing as you do that this
tested quality of your faith works out endurance."
(James 1:2, 3) Yes, we can have real joy if, under
opposition, we face up to the test of our faith.
Why? Because by enduring we uphold the side of
our heavenly Father in the great issue before all
the universe. Furthermore, God's Son assures us:
"By endurance on your part you will acquire your
souls." Yes, by endurance you will gain the reward
of life eternal.—Luke 21:16-19; 1 Peter 2:21-23;
2 Thessalonians 1:4, 5.

⁹ We live in the most blessed time of all human
history. Soon now Jehovah and his Son, Christ
Jesus, will rid the universe of all enemies of God's
kingdom. What a joy it will be, after that war, to
live under righteous conditions in the paradise
earth, free of suffering, sorrow and death! You
can have full confidence in that hope, because
"God . . . cannot lie." (Titus 1:2) Look ahead to
that blessed prospect, then, and never forsake the
worship of Jehovah the true God. Keep on in the
way of the truth, for "the world is passing away
and so is its desire, but he that does the will of
God remains forever."—1 John 2:17.

8. Why can we have real joy if we face up to the test of our
faith that opposition brings?
9. (a) Why are we living in the most blessed time of all human
history? (b) What joyful prospect is ahead for those who
never forsake the way of the truth?

"PRESS ON TO MATURITY"!

Now that you have considered some basic Bible truths, you need to continue in spiritual growth. So you will want to do as the apostle Paul advised: "Now that we have left the primary doctrine about the Christ, let us press on to maturity."—Hebrews 6:1.

To help you do just that, we strongly recommend that you read these two informative books:

"Things in Which It is
Impossible for God to Lie"

Life Everlasting—in
Freedom of the Sons of God

These practical Bible-study aids will help you to press on to maturity, as they bring you, among other things:

◆ Advanced knowledge and a richer understanding of God's Word of truth.

◆ A delightful synopsis of the entire Bible.

◆ Answers from the highest Authority to many of today's perplexing problems.

◆ A chart of Bible chronology revealing that few years remain for this present wicked system of things.

Each hardbound, 416 pages, beautifully illustrated

Both $1, or singly, 50c, postpaid

Write to **Watchtower**, using an address from the next page.

The Bible in Modern-Day English

The Bible translation most often quoted in this book is one in modern English. Did you observe how much easier it is to read? Ideas, once cloaked in archaic English, now shine out with meaningful brilliance. Its everyday language helps you to grasp information that is vital for gaining eternal life from its Great Author, Jehovah God. With understanding, too, comes new pleasure in delving into this storehouse of divine truth. You can obtain the **New World Translation of the Holy Scriptures** in the following editions:

REGULAR: Bound in green vinyl, with maps and concordance, 1,472 pages; mailed postpaid for only $1.

LARGE PRINT: 1,376 pages, valuable footnotes, appendix, concordance. $5 a copy.

DELUXE: Gold-edged pages with black or maroon flexible cover, $3.00 each.

POCKET: Flexible cover, $1.50 a copy.

Send your order to WATCHTOWER at any of these addresses:

ALASKA 99507: 2552 East 48th Ave., Anchorage. AUSTRALIA: 11 Beresford Road, Strathfield, N.S.W. 2135. BAHAMAS: Box N-1247, Nassau, N.P. BARBADOS, W.I.: Fontabelle Rd., Bridgetown. BELIZE: Box 257, Belize City. BRAZIL: Rue Guaíra, 216, Bosque da Saúde, 04142 São Paulo, SP. CANADA: 150 Bridgeland Ave., Toronto, Ont. M6A 1Z5. CONGO REPUBLIC: B.P. 2.114, Brazzaville. ENGLAND: Watch Tower House, The Ridgeway, London NW7 1RN. FIJI: Box 23, Suva. FRANCE: 81 rue du Point-du-Jour, 92100 Boulogne-Billancourt. GERMANY (WESTERN): Postfach 13025, 62 Wiesbaden-Dotzheim. GHANA: Box 760, Accra. GUYANA: 50 Brickdam, Georgetown 16. HAWAII 96814: 1228 Pensacola St., Honolulu. HONG KONG: 312 Prince Edward Rd., Second Floor, Kowloon. INDIA: South Avenue, Santa Cruz, Bombay 400054. INDONESIA: Jl Batuceper 47, Jakarta Pusat, DKI. IRELAND: 06 Lindsay Rd., Glasnevin, Dublin 9. JAMAICA, W.I.: 41 Trafalgar Rd., Kingston 10. KENYA: Box 47788, Nairobi. LEEWARD ISLANDS, W.I.: Box 119, St. Johns, Antigua. LIBERIA: P.O. Box 171, Monrovia. MALAYSIA: 20 Scotland Close, Penang. NEWFOUNDLAND, CANADA: 239 Pennywell Rd., St. John's. NEW ZEALAND: 621 New North Rd., Auckland 3. NIGERIA: P.O. Box 194, Yaba, Lagos State. PAKISTAN: 3-E Habibullah Rd., Lahore 3. PANAMA: Apartado 1386, Panama 1. PAPUA NEW GUINEA: Box 113, Port Moresby. PHILIPPINE REPUBLIC: 186 Roosevelt Ave., San Francisco del Monte, Quezon City D-503. RHODESIA: P.O. Box 1462, Salisbury. SIERRA LEONE: Box 136, Freetown. SOUTH AFRICA: Private Bag 2, P.O. Elandsfontein, Transvaal. SRI LANKA, REP. OF: 62 Layard's Road, Colombo 5. SWITZERLAND: Ulmenweg 45, P.O. Box 477, CH-3601 Thun. TRINIDAD, W.I.: 2 La Seiva Road, Maraval, Port of Spain. UNITED STATES OF AMERICA: 117 Adams St., Brooklyn, N.Y. 11201.